D0458644

 CREDO PERSPECTIVES

VOLUMES ALREADY PUBLISHED

 **CREDO PERSPECTIVES**

PLANNED AND EDITED BY

RUTH NANDA ANSHEN

Board of Editors

W. H. AUDEN

RICHARD COURANT

MARTIN C. D'ARCY, S.J.

RENÉ DUBOS

LOREN EISELEY

WERNER HEISENBERG

FRED HOYLE

MUHAMMAD ZAFRULLA KHAN

R. M. MACIVER

F. S. C. NORTHROP

SARVEPALLI RADHAKRISHNAN

ALEXANDER SACHS

JAMES JOHNSON SWEENEY

HARRY WOLFSON

AN INVITATION
TO HOPE

by POPE JOHN XXIII

Translated and arranged by

JOHN GREGORY CLANCY

Simon and Schuster, New York

Russell K. Nakata

ALL RIGHTS RESERVED
INCLUDING THE RIGHT OF REPRODUCTION
IN WHOLE OR IN PART IN ANY FORM
COPYRIGHT © 1967 BY SIMON & SCHUSTER, INC.
PUBLISHED BY SIMON AND SCHUSTER
ROCKEFELLER CENTER, 630 FIFTH AVENUE
NEW YORK, NEW YORK 10020
LIBRARY OF CONGRESS CATALOG CARD NUMBER: 67-11705
DESIGNED BY CECILE CUTLER
MANUFACTURED IN THE UNITED STATES OF AMERICA
FIRST PRINTING

CONTENTS

CREDO PERSPECTIVES:
Their Meaning and Function
RUTH NANDA ANSHEN

CREDO PERSPECTIVES

Their Meaning and Function

Credo Perspectives suggest that twentieth-century man is living in one of the world's most challenging periods, unprecedented in history, a dynamic period when he has almost unlimited choices for good and evil. In all civilizations of the world of our modern epoch, in both socialistic and capitalistic societies, we are faced with the compelling need to understand more clearly the forces that dominate our world and to modify our attitudes and behavior accordingly. And this will only happen if our best minds are persuaded and assembled to concentrate on the nature of this new epoch in evolutionary and moral history. For we are confronted with a very basic change. Man has intervened in the evolutionary process and he must better appreciate this fact with its influence on his life and work, and then try to develop the wisdom to direct the process, to recognize the mutable and the immutable elements in his moral nature and the relationship between freedom and order.

The authors in this series declare that science now permits us to say that "objective" nature, the world which alone is "real" to us as the one in which we all, scientists included, are born, love, hate, work, reproduce and die, is the world given us by our senses and our minds—a world in which the sun crosses the sky from east to west, a world of three-dimensional space, a world of values which we, and we alone, must make. It is true that scientific knowledge about macroscopic or subatomic events may enable us to perform many acts we were unable to perform before. But it is as inhabitants of this human world that we perform them and must finally recognize that there is a certain kind of scientific "objectivity" that can lead us to know everything but to understand nothing.

The symbol of *Credo Perspectives* is the Eye of Osiris. It is the inner eye. Man sees in two ways: with his physical eyes, in an empirical sensing or *seeing* by direct observation, and also by an indirect envisaging. He possesses in addition to his two sensing eyes a single, image-making, spiritual and intellectual Eye. And it is the *in-sight* of this inner Eye that purifies and makes sacred our understanding of the nature of things; for that which was shut fast has been opened by the command of the inner Eye. And we become aware that to believe is to see.

This series is designed to present a kind of intellectual autobiography of each author, to portray the nature and meaning of his creative process and to show the relevance of his work to his feelings and aspirations. In it we hope also to reflect the influence of the work on the man and on society, and to point to the freedom, or lack of freedom, to choose and pursue one profession rather than another. For the creator in any realm must surrender himself to a passionate pursuit of his labors, guided by deep personal intimations of an as yet undiscovered reality.

Credo Perspectives hope to unlock a consciousness that at first sight may seem to be remote but is proved on acquaintance to be surprisingly immediate, since it stems from the need to reconcile the life of action with the life of contemplation, of practice with principle, of thought with feeling, of knowing with being. For the whole meaning of *self* lies within the observer, and its shadow is cast naturally on the object observed. The divorce of man from his work, the division of man into an eternal and temporal half, results in an estrangement of man from his creative source, and ultimately from his fellows and from himself.

The hope of this series is to suggest that the universe itself is a vast entity where man will be lost if it does not converge in the person; for material forces or energies, or impersonal ideals, or scientifically objectified learning are meaningless without their relevance for human life and their power to disclose, even in the dark tendencies of man's nature, a law transcending man's arbitrariness.

For the personal is a far higher category than the abstract universal. Personality itself is an emotional, not an intellectual, experience; and the greatest achievement of knowledge is to combine the personal within a larger unity, just as in the higher stages of development the parts that make up the whole acquire greater and greater independence and individuality within the context of the whole. Reality itself is the harmony which gives to the component particulars of a thing the equilibrium of the whole. And while physical observations are ordered with direct reference to the experimental conditions, we have in sensate experience to do with separate observations whose correlation can only be indicated by their belonging to the wholeness of mind.

It is the endeavor of the authors to show that man has reached a turning point in consciousness, that his relationship with his creativity demands a clarification that can widen and deepen his understanding of the nature of reality. Work is made for man, not man for work. This series hopes to demonstrate the sacramental character of work, which is more easily achieved when the principal objects of our attention have taken on a symbolic form that is generally recognized and accepted; and this suggests a *law* in the relationship of a person and his chosen discipline: that it is valuable only when the spiritual, the creative, life is strong enough to insist on some expression through symbols. For no work can be based on material, technological, historical, or physical aspirations alone.

The human race is now entering upon a new phase of evolutionary consciousness and progress, a phase in which, impelled by the forces of evolution itself, it must converge upon itself and convert itself into one single human organism infused by a reconciliation of knowing and being in their inner unity and destined to make a qualitative leap into a higher form of consciousness that would transcend and complement individual consciousness as we know it, or otherwise destroy itself. For the entire universe is one vast field, potential for incarnation and achieving incandescence here and there of reason and spirit. And in the whole world of *quality* with which by the nature of our minds we necessarily make contact, we here and there apprehend pre-eminent value. This can be achieved only if we recognize that we are unable to focus our attention on the particulars of a whole without diminishing our comprehension of the whole, and of course, conversely, we can focus on the whole only by diminishing our comprehension of the particulars which constitute the whole.

The kind of knowledge afforded by mathematical physics ever since the seventeenth century has come more and more to furnish mankind with an ideal for all knowledge. This error about the nature of knowledge it is the hope of this series to expose. For knowledge is a process, not a product and the results of scientific investigation do not carry with them self-evident implications. There are now, however, signs of new centers of resistance among men everywhere in almost all realms of knowledge. Many share the conviction that a deep-seated moral and philosophical reform is needed concerning our understanding of the nature of man and the nature of knowledge in relation to the work man is performing, in relation to his *credo* and his life.

Credo Perspectives constitute an endeavor to alter the prevailing conceptions, not only of the nature of knowledge and work, but also of creative achievements in general, as well as of the human agent who inquires and creates, and of the entire fabric of the culture formed by such activities. In other words, this is an endeavor to show that what we see and what we do are no more and no less than what we are.

It is the endeavor of *Credo Perspectives* to define the new reality in which the estrangement of man from his work, resulting in the self-estrangement in man's existence, is overcome. This new reality is born through the reconciliation of what a man *knows* with what a man *is*. Being itself in all its presuppositions and implications can only be understood through the totality, through wholeness. St. Paul, who, like Isaiah before him, went into the market-place not to secularize truth but to proclaim it, taught man that the "new creation" could be explained only by conquering the daemonic cleavages, the destructive split, in soul and cosmos. And that fragmentation always destroys a unity, produces a tearing away from the source and thereby creates disunity and isolation. The fruit can never be separated from the tree. The Tree of Life can never be disjoined from the Tree of Knowledge for both have *one and the same* root. And if man allows himself to fall into isolation, if he seeks to maintain a self segregated from the totality of which he is a necessary part, if he chooses to be unrelated to the original context of all created things in which he too has his place—including his own labors—then this act of apostasy bears fruit in the demiurgical presumption of *magic,* a form of animism in which man seeks an authority of the self, placing himself above the law of the universe by attempting to separate the inseparable. He thus creates an unreal world after having destroyed or deserted the real. And in this way the method of analysis, of scientific objectivity, which is good and necessary in its right place, is endowed with a destructive power when it is allowed to usurp a place for which it is not fitted.

The naturalist principle that man is the measure of all things has been shattered more than ever in our own age by the question, "What is the measure of man?" Postmodern man is more profoundly perplexed about the nature of man than his ancestors were. He is on the verge of spiritual and moral insanity. He does not know who he is.

And having lost the sense of who and what he is, he fails to grasp the meaning of his fellow man, of his vocation and of the nature and purpose of knowledge itself. For what is not understood cannot be known. And it is this cognitive faculty which is frequently abrogated by the "scientific" theory of knowledge, a theory that refuses to recognize the existence of comprehensive entities as distinct from their particulars. The central act of knowing is indeed that form of comprehension which is never absent from any process of knowing and is finally its ultimate sanction.

Science itself acknowledges as real a host of entities that cannot be described completely in materialistic or mechanistic terms, and it is this transcendence out of the domain of science into a region from which science itself can be appraised that *Credo Perspectives* hope to define. For the essence of the ebb and flow of experience, of sensations, the richness of the immediacy of directly apprehended knowledge, the metaphysical substance of what assails our being, is the very act itself of sensation and affection and therefore must escape the net of rational analysis, yet is intimately related to every cognitive act. It is this increasing intellectual climate that is calling into birth once more the compelling Socratic questions, "What is the purpose of life, the meaning of work?" "What is man?" Plato himself could give us only an indirect answer: "Man is declared to be that creature who is constantly in search of himself, a creature who at every moment of his existence must examine and scrutinize the conditions of his existence. He is a being in search of meaning."

From this it is evident that there is present in the uni-

verse a *law* applicable to all nature including man and his
work. Life itself then is seen to be a creative process
elaborating and maintaining *order* out of the randomness
of matter, endlessly generating new and unexpected structures and properties by building up associations that quali-
tatively transcend their constituent parts. This is not to
diminish the importance of "scientific objectivity." It is,
however, to say that the mind possesses a quality that cannot be isolated or known exclusively in the sense of objective knowledge. For it consists in that elusive humanity
in us, our self, that knows. It is that inarticulate awareness that includes and *comprehends* all we know. It
consists in the irreducible active voice of man and is
recognized only in other things, only when the circle of
consciousness closes around its universe of events.

Our hope is to point to a new dimension of morality—
not that of constraint and prohibition but a morality that
lies as a fountainhead within the human soul, a morality
of aspiration to spiritual experience. It suggests that neces-
sity is laid upon us to infer entities that are not observed
and are not observable. For an unseen universe is necessary to explain the seen. The flux is seen, but to account
for its structure and its nature we infer particles of various
kinds to serve as the vertices of the changing patterns, placing less emphasis on the isolated units and more on the
structure and nature of relations. The process of knowing
involves an immaterial becoming, an immaterial identifica-
tion, and finally, knowledge itself is seen to be a dependent
variable of immateriality. And somewhere along this spiritual pilgrimage man's pure observation is relinquished and
gives way to the deeper experience of awe, for there can be

no explanation of a phenomenon by searching for its origin but only by discerning its immanent law—this quality of transcendence that abides even in matter itself. The present situation in the world and the vast accretion of knowledge have produced a serious anxiety which may be overcome by re-evaluating the character, kinship, logic and operation of man in relation to his work. For work implies goals and intimately affects the person performing the work. Therefore the correlation and relatedness of ideas, facts and values that are in perpetual interplay could emerge from these volumes as they point to the inner synthesis and organic unity of man and his labors. For though no labor alone can enrich the person, no enrichment can be achieved without absorbing and intense labor. We then experience a unity of faith, labor and grace which prepares the mind for receiving a truth from sources over which it has no control. This is especially true since the great challenge of our age arises out of man's inventions in relation to his life.

Thus *Credo Perspectives* seek to encourage the perfection not only of man's works but also and above all the fulfillment of himself as a person. And so we now are summoned to consider not only man in the process of development as a human subject but also his influence on the object of his investigation and creation. Observation alone is interference. The naïve view that we can observe any system and predict its behavior without altering it by the very act of observation was an unjustified extrapolation from Newton's *Celestial Mechanics*. We can observe the moon or even a satellite and predict its behavior without perhaps appreciably interfering with it, but we cannot do this with an amoeba, far less with a man and still less

with a society of men. It is the heart of the question of the
nature of work itself. If we regard our labors as a process of
shaping or forming, then the fruits of our labors play the
part of a mold by which we ourselves are shaped. And
this means, in the preservation of the identity of the knower
and the known, that cognition and generation, that is, creation, though in different spheres, are nevertheless alike.

It is hoped that the influence of such a series may help
to overcome the serious separations between function
and meaning and may show that the extraordinary crisis
through which the world is passing can be fruitfully met by
recognizing that knowledge has not been completely de-
humanized and has not totally degenerated into a mere
notebook overcrowded with formulas that few are able to
understand or apply.

For mankind is now engaged in composing a new theme.
Life never manifests itself in negative terms. And our hope
lies in drawing from every category of work a conviction
that nonmaterial values can be discovered in positive, af-
firmative, visible things. The estrangement between the
temporal and nontemporal man is coming to an end, community is inviting communion, and a vision of the human
condition more worthy of man is engendered, connecting
ever more closely the creative mind with the currents of
spiritual energy which breaks for us the bonds of habit
and keeps us in touch with the permanence of being
through our work.

And as, long ago, the Bearers of Bread were succeeded
by the Bearers of Torches, so now, in the immediacies of
life, it is the image of man and his vocation that can re-
kindle the high passion of humanity in its quest for light.

Refusing to divorce work from life or love from knowledge, it is action, it is passion that enhances our being.

We live in an expanding universe and also in the moral infinite of that other universe, the universe of man. And along the whole stretched arc of this universe we may see that extreme limit of complicity where reality seems to shape itself within the work man has chosen for his realization. Work then becomes not only a way of knowledge, it becomes even more a way of life—of life in its totality. For the last end of every maker is himself.

"And the places that have been desolate for ages shall be built in thee: thou shalt raise up the foundations of generation and generation; and thou shalt be called the repairer of the fences, turning the paths into rest."*

RUTH NANDA ANSHEN

---

* Isaiah, 58:12.

PROLOGUE

THE STRENGTH AND COLOR of John XXIII are usually made accessible to the reading public through theological and hagiological terms. To him are attributed, as the fertile center of his being, faith, charity, humility, or loving response to the will of God revealed in every event of his life.

But the most easily demonstrable quality of Angelo Giuseppe Roncalli's life was his almost unique ability to translate all of these supernatural qualities into direct, unselfconscious action that emanated from him as a person. His virtue did not emerge as a recognizable product of years of ascet-

ical campaigning against the world, the flesh and the
devil. It came out as something essentially ineluc-
table. To emphasize his possession of supernatural
endowments is to bestow on him a transcendental
character to which he himself would have made no
claim, even with all the self-confidence that Hannah
Arendt has seen in his *Journal of a Soul.* And it also
opens a chasm of "purely spiritual" unintelligibility
between the world and the most substantial and
specific human personality of recent years. His presence and action in the world have been the most
illustrious proof in the recent history of the Church
that supernature rests on nature, that Christian perfection means primarily a dynamic development of
the essentially human.

His presence and action have also been a needed
reassertion of the part of intuition in the human
power to know Christ, to know the Church, and to
know the nature and function of religion. The
Church for centuries has overstressed her intellectual rationale, and has assumed that men should
come to know her through instruction and polemics;
should even assess the power of example rational-
istically. But John saw each of the varied manifesta-
tions of his task with successive flashes of insight
and immediate sensibility. He would have called this
the inspiration of the Holy Spirit; he did so, indeed,
in accounting for his calling of an ecumenical council. And the inspiration of the Holy Spirit it surely

was, become visible in his calm, good-humored,
magnanimous and honest person.

Generations who have grown up in the ascetical
tradition of the Church have occasionally been told,
if not taught, that humility is truth. John's confidence in himself, far from needing to be explained
as existing in spite of, or alongside his humility, was
one of its products. Only the humble man could
have moved forward into the council, knowing that
time would substantiate his move, if only after his
death, and willingly risking the reasonable disap-
proval and logical criticism of the "prophets of
doom." It might well have been only the latter, always a source of pain and frustration to him, that
would be the sum of his personal harvest of the
work of the Council. His confidence, in this instance,
lay not so much in what he could do, but in the
rightness of his inspiration, in the "click" of that
moment of insight. Only the humble man can afford
to trust this kind of knowledge, which, because it
must live without discursive defense, is doubly vul-
nerable. In itself, and apart from the rumor that
attends it, it can become a Faustian exercise. "The
Devil," says Nietzsche, "is the oldest friend of insight." But even when it is energized by a pure heart,
it becomes a scandal to enemies and does not escape
calumny. John XXIII did not escape it. People who
return from contact with ecclesiastical cabals in
Rome still carry quotations from his critics—that

he was mad, and not with a divine madness; that his death saved the Church from untold abberations.

His freedom from personal ambition in ecclesiastical life was an evidence of the poverty of spirit to which he frequently refers in his *Journal of a Soul.* Overcoming the passion of ambition was not one of the needs of his design for Christian perfection. Because he possessed an original equanimity he was able to sustain himself on what Providence sent him. Christian thinking during the past several hundred years has come to set value only on what is won through struggle and conflict within the soul. Because of the general failure to esteem whatever is "merely" natural and human, Roncalli went from one obscure post to another, even becoming, in 1944, a branded obscurity who could be interpreted as a retaliation against the De Gaulle government by the papacy. If he suspected such an interpretation, he gives no hint of it in his *Journal.* To have put it aside or never to have known it—both are equal evidence of a profound innocence.

It has become a fond error of judgment and a consequent underestimation of John to invest the impact he had upon the world with a nimbus of mystery that happily cannot be explained. Once it is explained an oppressive responsibility settles on the mettlesome back of the modern Christian, and so we prefer to show ourselves breathless with adoration and impotence. For he was simply a man of untrammeled love.

If the Church had needed for centuries to be shown what the world expected of it, John came as the answer. It should be no mystery that a man physically unprepossessing, unintellectual, peasant in origin and appearance, who loved criminals and communists as well as the secure members of the Church "militant," who revealed signs of a pervasive sorrow at the breach among Christians, should have won an immediate and enduring response from the world at large. The figure of the simple, humble man who is open to all other men is a kind of archetype that many instructors of religion have held up bemusedly as an otherworldly ideal, to whose imitation they have exhorted the young, without facing the fact of the absence of living examples. So the figure had become a benign specter, part of the Christian dream, a trapped embryo as yet unrealized.

When Roncalli became Pope, the world outside the Roman Catholic Church was more prompt to recognize his qualities than Catholics were. Before his election, the man who is called Holy Father was in his own Church an immaculate stereotype; almost nothing was expected of him in the way of humanity. Few Catholics are put off by pomp and majesty or by aloofness of manner; thus few looked at this time for simplicity and direct, loving friendliness.

Even when they read these terms describing the new
Pope, they paid little attention, until they heard
more detached observers taking enthusiastic note.
The story of the Roman chambermaid who said to
Hannah Arendt, ". . . how could it happen that a
true Christian would sit on Saint Peter's chair? . . .
Had nobody been aware of who he was?" tells of
an unresolvable amazement which had accumulated
among closer witnesses, and which seems to con-
demn the predecessors of John less for positive failures against Christianity than for want of any
immediate feeling for it.

The qualities in a person of position which call
for a muted defense from advocates are a measure
of both subject and advocate. The compulsion to
shrug off elusively John's earthiness as opposed to
worldliness, and his want of intellectual attainment,
proves how unaccustomed the Christian world had
become to unaggressive forthrightness and to patient
readiness to declare the truth.

Speculative observers of the apparently revolutionary aspects of John's reign cannot help wondering
what silent and deep-buried reflections and images
fermented in his heart during his hidden life in the
limbo of Bulgaria, in Venice, in Istanbul. Even to
know them in part from his *Journal of a Soul* or in
the wider range of the present volume is to be left
in wonder at the moral and intellectual continence
of a man who was, in spite of apologetic shrugs, per-

ceptive and sensitive above the ordinary, and pragmatic as well. This continence became another affirmation greatly needed in the contemporary Church, for it was an emphasis on capacity rather than ability, and the *anima* as opposed to *animus*. It was a profession of a visceral faith in the sacredness of time and the process of ripening.

For the Church, as the spouse of Christ, is always in need of a witness to its feminine function. Yet during the ideological, social and economic revolutions of the nineteenth and earlier twentieth centuries, its movement had become ever more masculine in its emphasis on self-defense and on missionary offensive in non-Christian lands, where it took on the appearance of the companion of colonialism. Its task forces had grown in number and in centralized strength, and momentum had been established. John's spiritual instinct, however, was to receive, to expand, to open the Church rather than to direct it, to call home all its children. And he was happily not obsessed with those who refused to come, nor with the frenetic, task-charged devotees of the older Church.

Given a less fragmented, less self-conscious cultural context, John XXIII would have spoken in a symbolic idiom similar to that of John of the Cross and Francis of Assisi, both of whom thought it not weakness to speak of creation and the soul of man in terms of femininity. Perhaps the most baffling natural mystery about the life of John was that, confined to the trite spiritual vocabulary of the nineteenth and twentieth centuries, he was yet able to convey the finer comprehension of a more imaginative era in the spiritual history of the Church.

And he was himself the most eloquent exemplar of the ripening process in the economy of God. For after so many years out of the range of the central concerns of the Church, in silence and obscurity, his short reign became not at all an interim, as the electors are said to have supposed, but a focus, a culmination, and a turning point. His few years of public life thus assumed another characteristic of the life of Jesus, his professed model.

J.G.C.

I

THE NAME IS DEAR TO ME

The Pope Is New but the Line Is Ancient

W HEN, ON OCTOBER 28, 1958, the Cardinals of the Holy Roman Church chose me, in my seventy-seventh year, to be Pope of the whole Church of Christ, the conviction was widespread that I would be a transitional Pope. Instead, here I am now on the eve of the fourth year of my pontificate, in the midst of carrying out an extensive program, while the whole world watches.

Much has been written of me which far surpasses my merits. Allow me, if you will, to present myself to you as I see myself. I am like any other man who lives on this blessed earth. I have been endowed

with good health, and with sufficient common sense
to make it possible for me to see quickly to the
heart of things. My nature makes it easy for me to
love my fellow man, and thus it keeps me faithful
to the law of the Gospel. It obliges me to respect my
own rights and those of others and it keeps me from
doing evil to any man; rather, it encourages me to
do good to all.

My beginnings were humble indeed. I was raised
in poverty which was at once accepted and blessed,
which made few demands and which protected the
flowering of virtue and opened the way to a pursuit
of the lasting values of life.

Even today when I think of all the workers of
the world I still seek among them the faces of my
father, my brothers, themselves workers. I would
have been a laborer myself if the Lord had not
called me to another service. I would have been a
laborer as are my many nephews who, although they
have been to school, have wished to remain in the
fields to work or who, because the land will not support them all, have gone to factories and offices. I do
not in any way think myself diminished by saying
that my brothers are all workingmen, and that I am
the son of such a family.

From the time I was born I wanted nothing more
than to be a priest. And once a priest, I was content

to become a rural priest in my diocese. But Providence again chose to lead me in other paths. It called me away from my native village and led me on journeys through the countries of both East and West, confronting me with peoples of different religions and ideologies, leading me into contact with social problems of overwhelming dimension. Throughout it all, I have always sought to be a priest who is a shepherd and in so seeking I have been content. Thus, do not look for me to be a politician, a diplomat; seek rather the priest I am, the shepherd of souls, who acts among you in the name of the Lord.

Finally, my concern throughout my life has always been more with that which brings men together rather than with what separates them and raises division. And there you have me.

When, following my election to the responsibility of the Papacy, the Cardinal Dean of the Sacred College asked me by what name I wished to be known, I answered, "John," and then added a few words to explain why. The name is dear to me because it was the name of my father. It is a nostalgic name, too, for it is the name of the tiny parish in which I was baptized. It is a solemn name, for it is the name of many cathedrals, particularly of my own, the Church of the Lateran. It is a name that has been borne more often than any other in the long history of the Roman Pontificate. Twenty-two Popes were called John, and almost all of them led short lives. The last, John XXII, bishop of Avignon, lived six centuries ago. He governed the Church for eighteen years and died, a nonagenarian, in 1334. I would choose to hide my own insignificance within such an imposing array of pontiffs.

John was also the first name of Saint Mark the Evangelist, the pride and protector of my beloved Venice, whom Saint Peter, prince of the Apostles and first bishop of the Roman Church, loved as a son.

But there is an even more special reason for choosing the name John. It is the name of two men who were and are close to Christ. One of these men is John the Baptist, who went before the Lord. Not himself the Light, he bore witness to the Light—and indeed to truth, justice, and liberty—in his preaching, in his baptism, and in his death. The other is John the disciple and evangelist, loved by Christ and His mother, the same John who reclined at Jesus' side during the Last Supper and who drank deep of that love of which he was to be a burning and apostolic flame even to his old age.

May these two Johns ever announce to all the world this task of mine whereby I long "to prepare for the Lord a perfect people, to make straight his paths, that the crooked ways might be made straight and the rough ways smooth, that all mankind might see the salvation of God." May God in His goodness grant that, with the help of His grace, I, who have the same role as Peter, the first in this sovereign line, may reflect the same holiness of life and the same steadfastness of spirit; even, if it should please God, to the shedding of my blood.

When in 1952 Pope Pius XII unexpectedly asked me to become the patriarch of Venice, I told him that I did not need time to reflect before accepting the appointment. My will, in fact, had no role to play in this. I had no desire to be appointed to one office or ministry rather than to another. My episcopal motto was a sufficient reply: Obedience and Peace. And so, after thirty years in the direct service of the Holy See, I prepared myself to begin a new kind of life. I found myself shepherd of the flock of Venice, which I was to tend for the next six years, and I had reason once again to reflect on those words of the Psalm, "God bears our burdens." He supports us as we are and with what we possess; with His treasure in us and with our miseries.

This same thought was with me four years ago when I accepted the succession to the Chair of Peter, and it has been so in all that has followed

right up to the present. Since the Lord chose me,
unworthy as I am, for this great service, I feel I no
longer have any special ties in this life, no family, no
country or nation, nor any particular preferences
with regard to studies or projects, even good ones.
The whole world is my family. This awareness gives
meaning and tone to all that I do.

. I burn with love for all men, but I am conscious
also of the humility that the Gospel teaches. For I
know my own lowliness, raised by God to this high
office not because of any merits I possess, but according to His mysterious designs.

Vicar of Christ? I am not worthy to be called this.
I am the poor son of Battista and Marianna Roncalli, two good Christians, it is true, but modest and
humble. Vicar of Christ? Here, then, is my task: to
be priest and victim. The priesthood exalts me, but
the sacrifice that the priesthood demands makes me
tremble.

As I turn inward to myself and go back over the
various events of my life, I have to admit that up to
now the Lord has spared me those tribulations that
make the service of truth, justice, and charity difficult and unwelcome for so many. I passed through
infancy and boyhood without taking any notice of
poverty, without any family disturbances or trouble

with studies. Nor did I experience too many difficulties during my military service at the age of
twenty, and during World War I. Small and insig-
nificant as I was, I received nothing but a warm
welcome in the seminaries of Bergamo and Rome,
and during my ten years as secretary to my bishop
in my home town. Then from 1921 down to the
present: from Rome to Rome and finally to the
Vatican.

The warm welcome and the degree of affection
still shown by those who greet or approach me are
always a source of surprise to me. The maxim
"Know yourself" suffices for my spiritual serenity
and keeps me alert. The secret of my success must
lie there: in not "searching into things which are
above my ability" and in being content to be "meek
and humble of heart." The flattering words which
swirl around me cannot give rise in me to any delu-
sions concerning myself.

To the praise and best wishes of men I prefer the
mercy of the Lord who has chosen me for a task so
great that I desire Him to sustain me to the end of
my life. The little I know of myself and the sense of
my inadequacies does not allow me any self-infla-
tion. In the work imposed by obedience all my days
are happy and serene, even if there is always some

little annoyance. The Lord compensates for my small capacity, and I abandon myself completely to Him.

Experience has always taught me to fear responsibility. It is heavy enough in itself if assumed under obedience, but terrifying for whoever has sought it for himself, pushing himself forward without being called. Honors and distinctions, even in the ecclesiastical world, are "vanity of vanities." They assert the glory of a day; they threaten a man's salvation, and even from the point of view of human wisdom they are worth very little. Anyone who has lived in the midst of these stupidities as I did in Rome, and in the first ten years of my priesthood, can well insist that they deserve no better name.

I confess to being troubled by the variety of tasks which are my responsibility. Many men have described them to me in many ways. They propose them within the limits of their own inclinations, their own experience, and the perspective from which they view the life of individuals and society.

Some believe the Pope should busy himself in guiding the affairs of nations and that he should be a seasoned diplomat or a universal genius. They maintain that he should be wise in directing the day-by-day life of man, or that he should be the sort of

Pope whose spirit embraces all the advances of this modern age without exception. But they are not on the right track. They fashion an image of the Pope which is not consistent with sound thinking or the purpose of this office.

A new pontiff, in the trials of this life, is like the son of the patriarch Jacob who welcomed his grieving brothers and showed his love and compassion for them, saying, "I am Joseph . . . your brother."

I am not unaware that the new Pope is watched with friendship and warmth in some quarters and with uncertainty, even with hostility, in others, with everyone waiting to see what can be expected from him.

It is only natural that, among everyday activities which blend both the highest and the most ordinary activities of my office, observers will try to single out the most important, and perhaps the only distinctive feature of a pontificate which day by day is taking its place in history.

My sole concern is the good of souls, and my only wish is to see this pontificate meet the spiritual demands of the present time honestly and forcefully. I repeat, as vigorously and sincerely as possible, that my one desire is to be the shepherd, the pastor, of the whole flock. All other human gifts and accomplishments—learning, practical experience, diplomatic finesse—can broaden and enrich pastoral work, but they cannot replace it.

The sacred duty of the Pope is to purify all his intentions and to live in conformity with doctrine and with grace in such a way as to merit for himself the greater honor of growing to resemble Christ in grace, as His Vicar.

Over and above external activity, it is important to know the spirit and the policies by which things are done. No doubt, a pontificate takes its character from the Pope who conducts it and who gives it a particular personality. But it is evident that the Roman pontiffs through the centuries have reflected, or should have reflected, the face of Jesus Christ, the divine Master, who undertook his earthly journeys in order that He might sow the seed of divine learning and shed the light of good example.

There are certain words of the Gospel which are the focus and summation of all His teaching: "Learn from me, for I am meek and humble of heart." This is the great principle of gentleness and humility.

Insofar as my own person is concerned, I claim no special inspiration. I abide by the sound doctrine which teaches that everything comes from God.

My personal tranquillity which makes so great an impression on the world consists completely in this:

continuing in obedience as I always have, and not
desiring or praying to live longer, not even one day
beyond the time when the angel of death will come
to call me and take me to Paradise, as I am confident he will.

Above all, I am grateful to the Lord for the temperament he has given me, which preserves me from
anxieties and tiresome perplexities. I feel I am under
obedience in all things, and I have noticed that this
attitude, in great things and in small, gives me a
strength of daring simplicity that is wholly evangeli-
cal in nature.

I am naturally inclined toward compliance and a
readiness to appreciate the good side of people and
things, rather than to criticize and pronounce harsh
judgments. I am able to show friendliness to all and
forbearance, with courtesy and patience. Any kind
of distrust or discourtesy shown to anyone, especially to the humble, poor, or socially inferior, every
destructive or thoughtless criticism, makes me
writhe with pain. I say nothing, but my heart bleeds.

No matter how events may seem to be going
against the good of the Church, I must maintain
perfect serenity, which doesn't, of course, dispense
me from longing and from praying that His will may
be done on earth as it is in heaven.

Not to make predictions and not to give any as-

surances about the future is the rule of conduct that
comes from the spirit of tranquillity and of firmness
that the Pope, as the first among priests, must bestow upon the faithful and upon his fellow workers.

Another basic rule for the Pope's conduct is this
one of always resting content with his present state,
and not getting all tangled up with the future. Instead all should be left in the Lord's hands without
making too many plans for merely human action.

I remember my father. He had a large family.
"How will you support all of them?" he was asked.
He never worried. He used to say, "When I get up
in the morning and see the sun I think that for yet
another day the Lord will provide, even as He makes
the grass grow and feeds the birds."

I shall always speak the truth, but with mildness,
keeping silence about what might seem a wrong or
injury done to myself. The Lord sees everything and
will deal justly with me. Above all, I wish to continue always to render good for evil and in all things
to prefer the Gospel truth to the artifice of human
politics.

I leave to everyone else the superabundant cun-
ning and so-called skill of the diplomat. I will continue to be satisfied with my own bonhomie and
simplicity of feeling, word and behavior. In the end,

all turns out for the good of him who is faithful to the teaching and example of the Lord.

The love of the Cross must always be seen in me, a love which must win my heart more and more from the love of the things of this world. May it make me patient, equable, forgetful of self, always joyful. If I cannot do all the good that I think is necessary, I must not let myself be in the least worried or anxious. It is enough to do my duty in accordance with the promptings of charity. The Lord knows how to use everything for the triumph of his kingdom, even my not being able to do more. By work and example I must impart this tranquillity and peace to others.

A constant pain which is also a secret anxiety is the same old problem: not being able to keep up with all I have to do, and having to watch myself closely to try to overcome my natural indolence.

I must be particularly careful not to procrastinate, but to do at once what is most urgent. In everything, however, I must keep and impart to others that calm and composure with which alone things can be done and done properly. I will not worry if others are in a hurry. He who is always in a hurry, even in the business of the Church, never gets very far.

For the rest, I will continue to apply to myself what Cardinal Federigo Borromeo said of himself: "God knows my deficiencies, and the ones that I know too are enough to embarrass me."

II

MAN AND HIS PEACE

The Life of Every Century Has Need of
Great Forgiveness on the Part of God

THE FIRST GLORY of every pontificate
is its conformity to the Gospel command "Go and
teach." We who are men of God are not called simply to account for our individual lives. We must
likewise account for the state of the whole world.

Because of temperament and a long spiritual dis-
ciplining, for which I thank the Lord, I am not inclined to pessimism. I love to repeat what a recent
Pope was accustomed to say: I rejoice that I was
born to live now rather than in times past.

To the times that were I prefer the times that are.
Yet this dazzling world, this triumph of technol-

ogy, this glowing witness to a new wisdom, this new way of life which beclouds the serenity and tranquillity of the old ways, from time to time profoundly disturb me.

I know, I know, that the temptations of our time are many. They are a part of our inconstancy, of the impatience which expresses the imperfection of our intelligence; a part, too, of our vanity, our self-love, the vulnerability of our natures.

In any case the present is the only time that belongs to us. Therefore it is most precious to one who truly lives.

The wars that have convulsed our times, the harm resulting from false ideologies, and the great hardships and sufferings that too many have experienced for too long—all these have been a kind of warning. The scientific and technical progress that has given men the power to produce arms aimed at their own destruction has also given rise to anxiety and concern.

I know that the vision of these and other evils has disturbed some people to the point where they can see nothing but darkness and shadow over the world.

I prefer to place my trust in the Savior of the human race, who has not deserted those He has redeemed. As a matter of fact, in keeping with the advice of Christ the Lord, who urged us to recog-

nize the "signs of our times," we can, through all
the gloom, see a number of omens foretelling a better day for the Church and for mankind.

In the daily life of my office, I sometimes hear
opinions which disturb me. They are expressed by
people who, zealous though they may be, lack prudence and judgment in their evaluation of human
events. They can see nothing but calamity and dis-
aster in the present state of the world. Over and over
again they say that this modern age of ours, in com-
parison with past ages, is disintegrating.

I feel that I must disagree with these prophets of
doom who are always forecasting even worse dis-
asters, as though the end of the world were at hand.

The errors and faults of a human spirit that is
tempted to concentrate exclusively on enjoying the
results of modern scientific research should indeed
be deplored. But may God keep us from so exag-
gerating that we come to believe that His heavens
have closed over our heads, that darkness has fallen
over all the world, and that there is nothing left for
us to do but weep as we plod along.

Instead, we must take courage.

God has made men and nations curable!

The contacts I had in both the East and the West
convinced me—if, indeed, it was necessary—that
the world is small, and that for men of good will

there do not and there cannot exist barriers which are insurmountable.

God created men as brothers, not foes. The earth is for them to cultivate. Each and every man is made to enjoy the fruits of the earth and receive from it his sustenance and the necessities of life. The various nations are simply communities of men—that is, of brothers. They exist to work in brotherly cooperation for the common prosperity of human society, not simply for their own particular goals.

We are called brothers. We actually *are* brothers. We share a common destiny in this life and the next. Why, then, do we act as though we are enemies? Why do we envy one another? Why do we stir up hatred? Why do we prepare weapons for use against our brothers?

All the evils which poison men and nations and trouble so many hearts have a single cause and a single source, ignorance of the truth—and at times even more, a contempt for truth and a reckless rejection of it. Thus arise all manner of errors, which enter the recesses of men's hearts and the bloodstream of human society as would a virus. These errors subvert all order. They menace individuals and society itself.

Any heresy, old or new, proceeds from a false interpretation of the Gospel.

The eternal design of God the Creator centers in individual man, man raised from nothingness to likeness with Him, pierced by His very life. The abuse of human liberty upset tragically the original plan of God—but it did not halt His love for man. The Son of God becomes man to save man, to save the world, to penetrate it once again with His divine life, but this time in a manner beyond conception.

This fact, the Word of God made man and sacrificed for him, is the central fact of history. Twenty centuries prepare the way for Him, and twenty centuries receive light and life from Him.

In this modern period the face of the world has changed profoundly. It is hard for it to keep its balance between the attractions and the perils of a constant and almost exclusive pursuit of material goods, and in the midst of a total neglect or watering down of the spiritual principles that characterized the implanting and spread of Christian civilization through the centuries. The question before the Church in these times is not so much one of some particular point or other of doctrine or of discipline that has to be brought back to the pure fonts of Revelation and of tradition, as it is one of restoring the substance of human and Christian thinking and living to its full force.

Present indications are that the human family is
on the threshold of a new era.

All mankind is striving for a better future. I see
the awakening of mysterious forces.

Men are now more interested and concerned, they
are more ready to admit that their own abilities and
powers are limited. They long for peace, they are
weighing the things of the spirit. They are, finally,
however falteringly, mastering the process of social
development which marks a new era for society. It
is a development that impels individual men, classes
of society, and whole nations to work together more
and more and to offer each other the mutual help
that will complement each other's efforts.

For this reason, in response to an inner voice that
arose from a kind of heavenly inspiration, I felt that
the time was ripe to give the Catholic Church and
the whole human family the gift of a new Ecumenical Council.

Everything that the new Ecumenical Council is
intended to do aims at restoring to full splendor the
simple and pure lines that the face of the Church of
Jesus had at its birth, and at presenting it as its
divine founder made it: without blemish or wrinkle.

And yet this history has its darker side, too, a fact
which cannot be glossed over. These nineteen hun-

dred years have reaped their harvest of sorrow and
bitterness.

You know that God's Church has at times amid
the trials of the centuries lost some of its vigor, but
it has always found new strength again.

Its journey through the centuries is still a long
way from the point where it will be transported into
an eternity of triumph.

The critical issues, the thorny problems that await
men's solution, have remained the same for almost
twenty centuries. And why? Because the whole of
history and of life hinges on the person of Jesus.

And so the highest and noblest aim of the Ecumenical Council is to pause a little in a loving study
of the Church and try to rediscover the lines of its
more fervent youth; to reconstruct them in a way
that will reveal their power over modern minds.

I should like to say that I am expecting really
great things from this Council, which aims at bring-
ing back a greater vigor to faith, to doctrine, to
Church discipline, and to religious and spiritual life.
It seeks also to make a contribution toward reaffirm-
ing the principles of Christian law that serves as the
basis and the framework for the development of
civil, economic, political, and social life as well. The
law of the Gospel must reach the point where it

takes in and penetrates everything. This implies a participation on the part of all elements that make up the social order, working for a perfect fusion of the values of time and eternity.

The heritage of Christ must not be understood and applied in terms of the needs or demands of any one country or another, or on the basis of the shifting events of history, but rather with complete fidelity to the promises of Jesus, who has assured us of His presence for all time.

The Catholic Church is not an archaeological museum. It is the ancient village fountain that gives water to the generations of today, as it gave it to those of days gone by.

Our duty is not just to guard this treasure, as though it were some museum piece and we the curators, but to dedicate ourselves to the work that needs to be done in this modern age, following the path which the Church has followed for almost twenty centuries.

What is needed is that this doctrine be more widely known, more deeply understood, and more penetrating in its effects on men's moral lives. What is needed is that this certain and immutable doctrine be studied afresh and reformulated in contemporary terms. For the truths which are contained in our teaching are one thing; the manner in which these truths are set forth, with their meaning preserved intact, is something else.

Such is the aim of the Second Vatican Council. It musters the Church's best energies and studies how to make the message of salvation welcome among men. In doing so it opens a path that leads toward that unity of the human race which is so necessary if this earth of ours is to reflect heaven, "whose king is truth, whose law is love, whose duration is eternity."

The great desire, therefore, of the Catholic Church is to show itself to the world as gentle, patient and full of tenderness and sympathy. To the race of men, so oppressed by difficulty, it says what Peter once said to the poor man who begged an alms: "Silver and gold I have none; but what I have, that I give you. In the name of Jesus of Nazareth, arise and walk."

It will not be only the sons of the Catholic Church who will benefit, but all those brothers of ours who rejoice in the name of Christian, as well as those of ancient and glorious civilizations who do not know Christianity. Among them it will nurture and bring to fruition those seeds of religious faith and human progress which are already planted in their midst.

One final word. Love is all. Love is the foundation of civilization, love is the core of the message
of Christ to the world. In love is found the resolution of all social questions and political quarrels, for
Europe and for the world.

Love is the key.

III

SOCIAL PRINCIPLES

My NATURAL INCLINATION is to speak of doctrine with calmness and simplicity rather than loudly call attention to points of dissension and certain negative aspects in our thinking and our action. Such an inclination, however, does not divert me from the tremendous pastoral responsibility which is mine, nor lead me to ignore this or that point in Catholic doctrine which might not exactly caress the ear of the one who hears it.

Whoever, in whatever time, has responsibility for the care of souls, of families and of religious, civil, and social society, feels it an imperative duty to

51

oppose the landslide with which the three concupis-
cences threaten man and his existence. He feels,
further, the obligation to recall those ancient words,
so distasteful to some, which are words of invitation
to discipline and to penance.

It is with discipline and penance that social well-
being and peace can be attained.

Though the main goal toward which the Church
is striving is not an earthly one, still as it journeys
it cannot ignore the questions having to do with
temporal goods or pay no attention to the labors
that produce them. It is aware of the specific benefit
conferred on immortal souls by whatever serves to
make the lives of individual men a little more human. The Church realizes that when the light of
Christ shines upon men, they are helped to know
themselves better. Thus the Church leads them to
understand what they really are, what dignity they
enjoy, what goal they must pursue.

An outstanding example of the Church's social
teaching and concern is the superb encyclical *Rerum Novarum,* which my predecessor Leo XIII
gave to the world seventy years ago and in which
he voiced the Christian understanding of the rights
of the working class.

At the time he spoke the outlook that prevailed
on economic matters was one which for the most

part denied any correlation between economics and morality. Personal gain was considered the only valid motive for economic activity. In business, free and unrestricted competition was the rule. The laws of the market place determined profits and wages, interest on capital, prices of goods and services. The possibility of intervention by the state in economic matters was strictly guarded against. And as for trade unions, their status differed from country to country. They were either forbidden, tolerated, or acknowledged to possess strictly limited legal existence.

In such an economic world the power of the most influential and entrenched became itself the prevailing law and thus established domination over the ordinary business relationships between individuals, with a consequent undermining of the whole economic structure.

While the few grew increasingly richer, the masses of the working class found themselves trapped in conditions of severe hardship. Their wages could not buy them the necessities of life; even starvation threatened them. Their working conditions were such that their physical and spiritual health was under constant assault. Inhuman is the word for the working conditions to which women and children were sometimes subjected. And, to crown this human indignity, the specter of unemployment and the disintegration of family life haunted their daily lives.

Naturally, indignation and even rebellion were the response made by workers, and in their desperation they embraced extremist theories far worse in their effects than the evils they proposed to remedy.

It was at such a time and under pressure of such circumstances as these that Leo XIII wrote his encyclical, based on the needs of human nature itself and animated by the principles and spirit of the Gospel.

Here for the first time was a complete synthesis of social principles, formulated with such historical insight as to be of permanent value to Christendom. It is rightly regarded as a compendium of Catholic social and economic teaching.

There were those at the time who did not fail to accuse the Church of taking no interest in social matters other than to urge generosity on the rich and resignation on the poor. Leo XIII did not hesitate to set forth and defend the legitimate rights of the workers.

The basic economic and social principles for the reconstruction of human society concern first of all the nature of work. It is no mere commodity but a specifically human activity. For most men, their work is their livelihood. Thus their remuneration cannot depend exclusively on the state of the market. Justice and equity must play their roles in determining what it is to be. If they do not, then justice is violated no matter how freely both parties have entered into a contract for work.

Secondly, private ownership of property, including that of productive goods, is a natural right that the state cannot suppress. But such a right creates a social obligation to exercise it not only for one's own benefit but for the good of others as well.

As for the state, it has but one purpose: to assist the realization of the common good in the area of its temporal concern. Thus it cannot be indifferent to economic matters. Rather, its power must be used to assure the production of a sufficient supply of material goods. Its duty too is to protect the rights of all its people, and particularly the weaker among them, the workers, women and children. The state can never dispense itself or be dispensed from the obligation to help achieve a better condition of life and work for the workingman and his family.

Also in *Rerum Novarum,* Pope Leo affirmed the worker's natural right to join associations composed either of workers alone or of workers and employers, and pointed out that the associations should be structured in a way best calculated to safeguard the workers' legitimate professional interests. Nor may the worker be hindered in his right to work freely and on his own initiative within these associations for the achievement of these goals.

Finally, the relationship between workers and employers should be based on the principle of human solidarity and Christian brotherhood. The "liberal" tocsin of unrestricted competition and the Marxist creed of class warfare are clearly contrary to Christian teaching and to the nature of man.

These are the basic principles set forth by Leo in 1891. You can understand why *Rerum Novarum* is considered, even today, the Magna Charta of social and economic reconstruction.

In 1931, Pope Pius XI was not unaware that the face of the world had changed considerably since Pope Leo's encyclical. It was clear, for example, that free competition had been devoured by its own principles almost to the point of self-destruction. Great accumulations of wealth were concentrated in the hands of a few who, as Pius said, "for the most part are not the owners, but only the trustees and directors of invested funds, which they administer at their own good pleasure."

Thus, he added, "economic power has taken the place of the open market. An unrestrained appetite for domination has succeeded the desire for gain;

the whole economic regime has become hard, cruel and relentless in frightful measure." The state was becoming more and more the servant of an economic elite which continued to tighten its grasp on the economic enterprise of the whole world.

In his encyclical *Quadragesimo Anno* Pius XI made two points. First, he insisted that the primary law of economic life must not be the special interests of individuals or groups, nor unregulated competition, economic despotism, national prestige or imperialism, or any other aim of this sort; on the contrary, all forms of economic enterprise should be governed by the principles of social justice and charity. The second basic point was that a national and international structure of justice, affecting both the public and the private sector, must be established, within which all economic activity could be conducted not merely for private gain but also in the interests of the common good.

In the thirty years which have passed since then, the economic scene has undergone a radical transformation, both in the internal structure of the various nations and in their relations with one another.

In the field of science, technology, and economics there is the discovery of nuclear energy, first used for purposes of war and later employed for peaceful ends. Chemistry possesses almost unlimited potential in the production of synthetic materials. There is, too, the growth of automation in industry and public services; the modernization of agriculture; the easing of communications, especially by radio and television; faster transportation; and the initial conquest of interplanetary space.

In the social field we have the development of social insurance, and in the more economically advanced countries social-security systems have been introduced. Workers in labor unions are assuming greater responsibility for the solution of major social and economic problems. Basic education continues to improve; a wider distribution of essential commodities, greater opportunities for advancement in industry and the consequent breaking down of class barriers, and a greater interest in world affairs shown by people of average education—all of these are fairly contemporary changes in the social picture of the world's communities.

At the same time, however, this assessment serves to bring to light certain glaring discrepancies. There is, in the first place, an increasing lack of balance between agriculture and industry and public services in most nations. Secondly, there are areas of varying economic prosperity within the same political communities. Finally, with a global perspective

one sees a marked disparity in the economic wealth
possessed by different countries.

In the political field there have been many changes.
In a number of countries all classes of citizens share
in the public life of their nation, and public authorities become increasingly concerned with social and
economic matters. We see, too, the gradual disap-
pearance of colonialism and the attainment of political independence by the peoples of Asia and Africa.
More and more, nations, aware of common needs,
are depending on one another. There is, moreover,
a wide network of societies and organizations whose
vision is supranational and which concentrate on the
economic, social, cultural, and political welfare of
all nations throughout the world.

As I pass all this in review, I am aware of my
responsibility to take up the torch which my great
predecessors lighted. All who would seek solutions
to the many social problems of our times may find
illumination here. My purpose, therefore, is to confirm and make more specific the teaching of my
predecessors, and to determine clearly the mind of
the Church on the new and important problems of
the day.

I should point out that in the economic order first
place must be given to the personal initiative of pri-

vate citizens working either singly or with each other
in various ways for the attainment of common purposes.

But, for reasons explained by my predecessors,
the state has a role to play, too, in the economy, in
a way suitable to the promotion of social progress
and the well-being of all citizens.

Its task is one of directing, stimulating, coordinat-
ing, supplying and integrating. Its guiding principle
in all this must be the "principle of subsidiary function" formulated by Pius XI in *Quadragesimo Anno:*
"There is a fixed and unchangeable principle of social philosophy which states that while it is wrong
to withdraw from the individual and commit to a
community what private enterprise and industry can
accomplish, so too it is an injustice, a grave evil
and a disturbance of right order, for the larger and
more powerful community to arrogate to itself functions which can be performed efficiently by smaller
and less important units of society. Of its very nature
the true aim of all social activity should be to help
members of the social body, but never to destroy
or absorb them."

With the present advance in scientific knowledge
and productive technology, the state has a greater
power than ever before to reduce imbalances which
may exist between different branches of the econ-

omy or between different regions within the same
country or even between the different peoples of the
world. So, too, it has a greater ability to control
fluctuations in the economy and to provide effective
measures for preventing the recurrence of mass unemployment. Thus there is pressure on those in
authority, responsible as they are for the common
good, to increase the degree and scope of their activities in the economic sphere, and to devise the ways
and means and set the necessary machinery in mo-
tion to attain this end.

A word of warning, however: The influence of
the state on the economy, wide and penetrating
though it be, must never be used to deprive the individual citizen of his freedom of action. Rather, it
must increase his freedom while effectively guaran-
teeing the protection of his essential personal rights.
Among these is his right and his duty to be the one
primarily responsible for his own upkeep and that
of his family. Hence every economic system must
allow and assist the free development of productive
activity.

One of the chief characteristics of our age is an
increase in social relationships. These have led to
the introduction of many and varied forms of associations into the lives and activities of citizens, and
to their acceptance within our legal framework. Sci-

entific and technical progress, greater productive
efficiency, and a higher standard of living have all
contributed to this trend.

Such development has also activated the increased intervention of the state, even in areas of
intimate concern to the individual, such as health
and education, the choice of career, and the care
and rehabilitation of the physically and mentally
handicapped.

There is consequently a multiplicity of restrictive
laws and regulations in many departments of human
life. It follows that the sphere of a person's freedom
of action is diminished. The means used, the methods followed, the atmosphere created, all conspire
to make it difficult for a person to think independ-
ently, to act on his own initiative, exercise his
responsibility, and express and fulfill his own personality. What follows? Do these increased social
relationships necessarily reduce men to being mere
automatons? By no means.

None of this growth in the social life of man is
a product of natural forces working by blind impulse. It is men who have done it all, men who are
free and independent by nature, but who also must
recognize and obey the laws of economic development and social progress, and who cannot altogether
escape the pressure of their environment.

It follows that those who hold public office must have a sane view of the common good. They must weigh all those social conditions which favor the full development of human personality. Moreover, it is vital that the various subordinate structures of society through which this social growth is expressed be really autonomous, and cooperate in the pursuit of their own specific interests and those of the common good. These groups must themselves present the form and substance of a true community, and this will happen only if they treat their individual members as human persons and encourage them to take an active part in the ordering of their lives.

IV

WORK AND THE WORKER

I AM PROFOUNDLY saddened by the unhappy sight of millions of workers in many countries and even entire continents who are condemned to live with their families in subhuman conditions because of inadequate wages. In most of these countries the process of industrialization is only in its initial stages, or is still not sufficiently developed.

Nevertheless, in some of them the wealth and luxury of the privileged few stands in arrogant, offensive contrast to the utter poverty of the vast majority. In some parts of the world men are crushed by unspeakable privations so that the rate of economic

growth of the country can be increased more rapidly than would be possible if social justice and
equity were considered. In other countries a high
percentage of the national income is directed to
building up the national image, with vast sums being spent on armaments.

In countries which are economically more developed, relatively unimportant and relatively valueless
services are disproportionately rewarded, while the
diligent and profitable work of whole classes of
honest, hard-working men gets small reward. Their
rate of pay is quite inadequate to meet the basic
needs of life. In no way does it correspond to the
contribution they make to the good of the community, to the profits of the company for which they
work, and to the general national economy.

In the light of all this, I consider it my duty to
assert that the wages for work done is not something
that can be left to the laws of the market place; nor
should it be a decision left to the will of the more
economically entrenched. It must be determined in
accordance with justice and equity. This means quite
simply that workers must be paid a wage which
allows them to live a truly human life and to fulfill
their family obligations with dignity.

To determine what a just wage is, other factors
must be considered. There is the effective contribu-

tion which each individual makes to the economic effort, the financial state of the company for which he works, the demands of the general good of his own country—weighing carefully the impact on the over-all employment of the working force in the country as a whole—and, finally, the requirements of the common good of the universal family of nations, both large and small.

In view of the rapid expansion of national economies, particularly since the war, there is one very important social principle that should be emphasized. It is this: social progress must keep pace with economic progress, so that all classes of citizens can participate in the increased productivity. Extreme vigilance and effort is needed to ensure that social inequalities, far from increasing, are reduced to a minimum.

It is important, too, that moral progress should not lag behind economic progress. Anything else would be unworthy of men, not to say of Christians. If the working classes have an abundance of material goods and enjoy all the benefits of civilization while losing or neglecting those higher goods which pertain to the immortal soul, what does it profit them?

The economic prosperity of a nation is not so

much its total assets in terms of wealth and property as it is the equitable division and distribution of this wealth. This guarantees the personal development of the members of society, which, after all, is the true goal of a nation's economy.

In this connection the system of self-financing adopted in many countries by large, or comparatively large, firms should be noted. Because these companies are financing replacement and plant expansion out of their own profits, they grow rapidly. In such cases, the workers should receive shares in the firm for which they work, especially when they are paid no more than a minimum wage.

Here again a quotation from Pius XI is pertinent: "It is entirely false to ascribe to the property alone or to the work alone whatever has been obtained through their combined efforts. And it is unjust for either, denying the efficacy of the other, to arrogate to itself whatever has been produced."

Experience suggests many ways in which the demands of justice can be satisfied. One I would mention: It is especially desirable, I think, that workers gradually come to share in the ownership of their company, by ways and in the manner that seem most suitable.

There is another point: Any adjustment between

wages and profits must take into account the demands of the common good of the particular country and of the whole human family.

I would list some of these. On the national level
they include employment of the greatest possible
number of workers; care lest privileged classes arise,
even among the workers; a balance between wages
and prices; the need to make goods and services
accessible to the greatest number; elimination, or
at least restriction, of inequalities in the various
branches of the economy—that is, between agriculture, industry and services; creation of a proper
balance between economic expansion and the development of social services, especially through the
activity of public authorities; the best possible adjustment of the means of production to the progress
of science and technology; seeing to it that the
benefits which make possible a more human way of
life will be available not merely to the present generation but to the coming generations as well.

On an international level, these would include
the avoidance of unfair competition between the
economies of different countries; the building up of
mutual collaboration and good will; and the effective cooperation of all in the development of economically less privileged communities.

An interesting aspect of human activity today is

that people are aiming at proficiency in their trade or profession rather than at the acquiring of private property. An income derived from hard work and the rights consequent upon work is esteemed more highly than one that derives from capital and the rights of capital.

This is as it should be. Work, as the immediate expression of a human personality, must always be rated higher than the possession of goods, which of their very nature are merely instrumental. This view of work is certainly an indication that an advance has been made in our civilization.

In the light of this change, is man's natural right to own private property no longer operative? Has it lost some or all of its validity in view of these economic conditions I have been discussing?

The answer is a simple no. The right of private ownership of goods, including productive goods, is always valid. It is part of the natural order, which teaches that the individual is prior to society and that society must be ordered to the good of the individual.

Moreover, it would be senseless to insist on free personal initiative in the economic field and at the same time deny man's right to dispose freely of the means indispensible to achieving it.

Besides, both history and experience testify that

in those states which do not recognize the rights of private ownership of goods, the productive included, freedom in almost every other direction is suppressed. Surely this suggests that the exercise of freedom finds its guarantee and incentive in the right of ownership.

But in saying all this it is not enough to assert that the right to own private property and the means of production is inherent in human nature. This right must be extended in practice to all classes of citizens.

Because of the rapid development of an increasing number of nations, this is the time to insist on a more widespread distribution of property. The state can do this by employing various techniques of proved efficiency, by pursuing an economic and social policy which facilitates the widest possible distribution of private property in terms of durable consumer goods, houses, lands, tools and equipment (in the case of craftsmen and owners of family farms), and shares in the medium and large business concerns. This policy is in fact being pursued with considerable success by several of the socially and economically advanced nations.

State and public ownership of property continues to increase. The common good demands that public authority broaden its sphere of activity. But here too the "principle of subsidiary function" must be observed. The state and other agencies of public law must not extend their ownership beyond what is clearly required by considerations of the common good, and even then there must be safeguards. Otherwise, private ownership could be sharply reduced, or, worse, completely destroyed.

It is undeniable that many people are moving from their farms into more congested areas as well as into the cities themselves. This is a shifting of population that is going on in nearly every part of the world, often on a large scale. There are complex human problems involved, and their solution is difficult.

As an economy develops, the number of people engaged in agriculture decreases, while the percentage employed in industry and the various services rises. There are reasons, however, for the shift in population other than purely economic ones. Among these is the desire to escape from a constricted way of living that offers little prospect of a more comfortable way of life. The lure of novelty and adventure, the prospect of easy money, of greater freedom and the enjoyment of all the amenities of town and city life are all factors. Contributory to all of these is doubtless the fact that farming has become a de-

pressed occupation. It is inadequate both in productive efficiency and in the standard of living it
provides.

The fundamental problem that all of this poses
confronts most countries today. What can be done
to reduce the disproportion in productive efficiency
between agriculture on the one hand and industry
and services on the other? What can be done to
guarantee agricultural living standards that will ap-
proximate as closely as possible those enjoyed by
city dwellers who draw their resources either from
industry or from the services in which they are
engaged? What can be done to persuade agricultural
workers that, far from being inferior, they have
every opportunity of developing their personality
through their work, and can look forward to the
future with confidence?

In the first place, much thought must be given,
especially by public authorities, to the suitable development of essential facilities in country areas—
such as roads; transportation; means of communi-
cation; drinking water; housing; health services;
elementary, technical and professional education;
religious and recreational facilities; and the supply
of modern installations and furnishings for farm
homes. Such services as these are necessary nowa-

days if a becoming standard of living is to be maintained.

The economic development of a country must take place gradually, with an even balance between all sectors of the economy hopefully maintained. Agriculture, therefore, must be allowed to make use of the same reforms in the method and type of production and in the conduct of its business as are permitted or required in the economic system as a whole. All such reforms should correspond as nearly as possible to those introduced in industry and the various services.

In addition, a sound agricultural program is needed if balanced progress in the various branches of the economy is to be accomplished. This must take into account tax policies, credit, social insurance, prices, the fostering of ancillary industries and the adjustment of the structure of farming as a business enterprise.

As for social insurance, the existence of two forms may be necessary: one concerned with agricultural produce, the other with the farm workers and their families. I realize that agricultural workers earn less per capita than workers in industry and the services, but that is no reason to consider it socially just to set up systems of social insurance in which the allowances of farm workers and their families are substantially lower than those of other classes of workers. Insurance programs that are established for the general public should not differ markedly whatever be the economic sector in which the individuals work or obtain their income.

Systems of social insurance and social security can make a most effective contribution to the overall distribution of national income in accordance with the principles of justice and equity. They can therefore be instrumental in reducing imbalances between the different classes of citizens.

Given the special nature of agricultural produce, modern economists must devise a suitable means of price protection. Ideally, such price protection should be enforced by the interested parties themselves, though supervision by the public authority cannot be altogether dispensed with.

Among citizens of the same political community there is often a marked degree of economic and social inequality. The main reason for this is that they are living and working in different areas, some of which are more economically developed than others.

Where this situation exists, justice and equity demand that public authority try to eliminate or reduce such imbalances. It should ensure that the less devel-

oped areas receive such essential public services as
their circumstances require, in order to bring the
standard of living in these areas into line with the
national average. Furthermore, a suitable economic
and social policy must be devised which will take
into account the supply of labor, the drift of population, wages, taxes, credit, and the investing of
money, especially in expanding industries. In short,
it should be a policy designed to promote useful
employment, creative initiative, and the exploitation
of local resources.

But the justification of all government action is
the common good. Public authority, therefore, must
bear in mind the interests of the nation as a whole.
This means that it must promote all three areas of
production—agriculture, industry, and services—
simultaneously and evenly. Everything must be done
to ensure the treatment of citizens of the less developed areas as responsible human beings, permitting
them to play the major role in achieving their own
economic, social, and cultural advancement.

Probably the most difficult problem today concerns the relationship between political communities
that are economically advanced and those in the
process of development. The solidarity that binds all
men together as members of a common family
makes it impossible for wealthy nations to look with

indifference upon the hunger, misery, and poverty of other nations whose citizens cannot enjoy even elementary human rights. With the nations of the world becoming more and more dependent on one another, It will not be possible to preserve a lasting peace so long as glaring economic and social imbalances persist.

Justice and humanity demand that those countries producing consumer goods, especially farm products, in excess of their own needs should come to the assistance of other countries where large sections of the population are suffering from want and hunger. It is nothing less than an outrage to justice and humanity to destroy or to squander goods that other people need for their very lives.

Of itself, however, emergency aid will not go far in relieving want and famine when these are caused —as they so often are—by the primitive state of a nation's economy. The only permanent remedy for this is to make use of every possible means to provide these citizens with the scientific, technical, and professional training they need, putting at their disposal the necessary capital for speeding up economic development with the help of modern methods.

The developing nations, obviously, have certain unmistakable characteristics of their own, resulting from the nature of the particular region and the natural dispositions of their citizens, with their time-honored traditions and customs.

In helping these nations, therefore, the more advanced communities must recognize and respect this individuality. They must beware of making the assistance they give an excuse for forcing these people into their own national mold.

There is also a further temptation which the economically developed nations must resist: that of giving technical and financial aid with a view to gaining political control in the poorer countries and furthering their own plans for world domination.

Let me be quite clear on this point. A nation that acted from these motives would in fact be introducing a new form of colonialism—cleverly disguised, no doubt, but actually reflecting that older, outdated type from which many nations have recently emerged. Such action would, moreover, have a harmful impact on international relations and would constitute a menace to world peace.

V

"I PRAY NOT THAT YOU TAKE THEM OUT OF THE WORLD, BUT THAT YOU KEEP THEM FROM EVIL"

SCIENTIFIC AND TECHNICAL progress, economic development, and the betterment of living conditions are certainly valuable elements in a civilization. But we must realize that they are essentially instrumental in character, and not supreme values in themselves.

It pains me, therefore, to see how completely indifferent to the true scale of values are so many people in the economically developed countries. Spiritual values are ignored, forgotten, or denied, while the progress of science, technology, and economics is pursued for its own sake, as though mate-

rial well-being were the be-all and end-all of life.
This attitude is contagious, especially when it in-
fects the work that is being done for the less developed countries, which have often preserved in their
ancient traditions a sharp, vital awareness of the
more important human values on which the moral
order rests.

Individual political communities may indeed enjoy a high degree of culture and civilization. They
may have a large and industrious population, an
advanced economic structure, great natural resources, and extensive territories. Yet, even so, in
isolation from the rest of the world they are virtu-
ally incapable of finding an adequate solution to
their major problems. Nations, therefore, must work
with each other for their mutual development and
perfection. They can help themselves only insofar as
they succeed in helping one another. That is why
international understanding and cooperation are so
necessary.

Yet although individuals and nations are becoming more and more convinced of this twofold neces-
sity, it would seem that men in general, and particularly those with high responsibility in public life,
are showing themselves incapable of achieving it.
The root of such inability is not to be sought in
scientific, technical, or economic reasons, but in the

absence of mutual trust. Men, and consequently nations, live in fear of each other. Each fears that the other harbors plans of conquest and is waiting only for a favorable moment to execute these plans. Hence each organizes its own defense and builds up armaments as a deterrent against the would-be aggressor.

The result is a vast expenditure of human energy and natural resources on projects which are disruptive of human society rather than beneficial to it. And all the while a growing uneasiness gnaws at men's hearts and makes them less responsive to the call of nobler enterprises.

The root cause of so much mistrust is the presence of ideological differences between nations, and more especially between their leaders.

Both sides speak of "justice" and "the demands of justice," but these words frequently assume different or opposite meanings according to which side uses them. Hence, when rulers of nations appeal to justice and the demands of justice, they not only disagree on terms, but often increase the tension that exists between their states. And so the belief is engendered that if a nation is to assert its rights and pursue its own interests, there is only one way open to it: to have recourse to violence—ignoring the fact that violence is the source of the very greatest evils.

Mutual trust among rulers of states cannot begin or increase except by recognition of and respect for the moral order.

But the moral order has no existence except in God; cut off from God it must necessarily disintegrate. Moreover, man is not just a material organism. He is also spirit, endowed with reason and freedom. He demands, therefore, a moral and religious order; and it is this order—and not considerations of a purely extraneous, material order—which has the greatest validity in the solution of the problems of his life as an individual and as a member of society, and problems concerning individual states and their interrelations.

It has been claimed that in an era of scientific and technical triumphs such as ours man can well afford to rely on his own powers, and can construct a high civilization without God. But the truth is that these very advances in science and technology frequently involve the whole human race in such difficulties as can be solved only in the light of a sincere faith in God, the Creator and Ruler of man and his world.

The almost limitless horizons opened up by sci-

entific research only tend to confirm this truth.
More and more men are beginning to realize that
science has so far done little more than scratch the
surface of nature and reality. There are hidden
depths still to be explored and adequately explained.
Such men are appalled when they consider how
these gigantic forces for good can be turned by science into instruments of destruction. They realize
then the supreme importance of spiritual and moral
values if scientific and technical progress is to be
used in the service of civilization and is not to involve the whole human race in irremediable dis-
aster.

The most fundamental modern error is that of
imagining that man's natural sense of religion is
nothing more than the outcome of feeling or fantasy,
to be eradicated from his soul as an anachronism
and an obstacle to human progress. And yet this
very need for religion reveals a man for what he is:
a being created by God and tending always toward
God.

Whatever the technical and economic progress of
the world, there will be no peace or justice until
men find their dignity as creatures and sons of God,
Who is the first and final cause of all created being.
Separated from God a man is but a monster, in him-

self and toward others; for the right ordering of human society presupposes the right ordering of man's conscience with God, Who is Himself the source of all justice, truth, and love.

The transition from theory to practice is of its very nature difficult; and it is especially so when one tries to reduce to concrete terms a social doctrine such as that of the Church. There are several reasons why this is so; among them I can mention man's deep-rooted selfishness, the materialism in which modern society is steeped, and the frequent difficulty of determining the demands of justice in a given instance.

Consequently, a purely theoretical instruction in man's social and economic obligations is inadequate. People must also be shown ways in which they can properly fulfill these obligations.

In His prayer for the Church's unity, Christ did not ask His Father to remove His disciples from the world: "I pray not that You take them out of the world, but that You keep them from evil." No man, therefore, should imagine that a life of activity in the world is incompatible with spiritual perfection. The two can very well be harmonized. It is a gross error to suppose that a man cannot perfect himself except by putting aside all temporal activity, on the plea that such activity will inevitably lead him to compromise his personal dignity as a human being and as a Christian.

It is perfectly in keeping with the plan of divine Providence that a man should develop and perfect himself through his daily work, which, in most cases, is of a secular nature. Here is the task of the Church today: to humanize and to Christianize this modern civilization of ours. The continued development of this civilization, indeed its very survival, insists that the Church do its part in the world.

Wherever artistic and philosophical values exist which are capable of enriching the culture of the human race, the Church fosters and supports them. It does not identify itself with any one culture—not even with European and Western civilization, although its history is closely intertwined with that civilization—for its mission pertains chiefly to matters which are concerned with religion and the eternal salvation of men. But the Church is full of youthful vigor and is constantly renewed by the breath of the Holy Spirit, and so it is willing at all times to recognize, welcome, and even assimilate anything that redounds to the honor of the human mind and heart, whether or not it originates in parts of the world washed by the Mediterranean Sea,

which from the beginning of time was destined by
God's Providence to be the cradle of the Church.

The sheer number of Christians means little if
they lack virtue; if, while enjoying the name of
Catholic, they do not stand firm in their purpose; if
their spiritual life does not flourish; if, after being
reborn to divine grace, they do not excel in that
spirit of vigorous and sensible youthfulness which is
always ready to perform generous and useful deeds.
Their profession of faith must not only be a statistic
in a census, it must create a new man and give all
his actions a supernatural strength, inspiring, guiding, and controlling them.

The words of our divine Master are true for all
time: "Seek therefore first the kingdom of God and
His justice; and all these things shall be added unto
you." The man who is "light in the Lord" and who
walks as a "child of light" has a sure grasp of the
fundamental demands of justice in all life's difficulties and complexities, obscured though they may be
by so much individual, national, and racial selfishness.

Animated, too, by the charity of Christ, he finds
it impossible not to love his fellow men. He makes
their needs, their sufferings, and their joys his own.
There is a sureness of touch in all his activity in

every field. It is energetic, generous, and considerate. For "Love is patient, is kind; love is not envious, or boastful, is not arrogant. Love is not ambitious. It does not rejoice at wrong, but rejoices in the truth. Love bears all things, believes all things, hopes all things, endures all things."

VI

THE INDIVIDUAL AND THE PERSON

A SHORT TIME AGO, I, as a successor to Saint Peter, still trembled under the first awareness of the mission conferred on me as pastor of the Universal Church. I was still somewhat shy about the name of John which I had chosen in token of a good will that was at once anxious and firm with regard to the program for preparing the ways of the Lord. Suddenly I thought of the valleys to be filled and the mountains to be brought low, and I began to advance on my way. And then, day by day, I came to recognize in great humility of spirit that truly the hand of the Most High was with me. The

87

sight of the crowds who from every part of the world gathered here in Rome or at Castelgandolfo to greet me, to hear me, and to seek my blessing was constant and touching.

My task is to "prepare for the Lord a perfect people," which is exactly like the task of the Baptist, who is my patron and from whom I take my name. And it is not possible to imagine a higher and more precious perfection than that of the triumph of Christian peace. It is a peace of heart, peace in the social order, in life, in well-being, in mutual respect, and in the brotherhood of all nations.

The message of peace is the very beat of my heart, the heart of a father and of a bishop of the Holy Church. May I even grow weary of my own eloquence in announcing it.

In order that any association of men in society be strongly structured and productive, one fundamental principle must be recognized: each individual man in that society is a person. He has intelligence and free will and consequently rights and duties. These are universal, inviolable, and wholly inalienable.

What are his rights? Man has the right to live. He has a right to whatever is necessary for the development of life, particularly food, clothing, shelter, medical care, rest, and, finally, the necessary social services. Thus, he has the right to be cared for if he is ill, or if he suffers disability stemming from his work; so too in widowhood, in old age; and during enforced unemployment—in short, any time when through no fault of his own he is deprived of his means of livelihood.

Man has the right to be respected. He has a right to his good name. He has a right to seek freely for truth. His right extends, further, within the limits of the moral order and the common good, to freedom of speech and publication, and the freedom to follow whatever profession he may choose. He has the right, also, to accurate public information.

He has the right to share in the wider knowledge of his time, and thus to receive a good general education, and a technical or professional training consistent with the degree of educational development in his own country.

Furthermore, gifted members of society should be able to engage in more advanced studies, that they might, as far as possible, occupy positions of responsibility in keeping with their natural talent and acquired skill.

Also among man's rights is that of being able to worship God according to his own conscience, and to profess his religion both in private and in public. Human beings also have the right to choose for themselves the kind of life which appeals to them.

In the economic sphere, it is evident that a man has the inherent right not only to be given the opportunity to work, but also to be free to exercise personal initiative in the work he does.

The conditions in which a man works are a corollary to these rights. They must not be such as to weaken his physical or moral fiber or to hinder the proper growth of adolescents into manhood.

Man's dignity gives him the right to take part in economic activities suitable to his capacity and responsibility; to own property, including productive goods; and to join with his fellows in associations and to structure these in whatever way will help them gain their objectives.

Again, every human being has the right to freedom of movement and of residence within his own country. And when there are just reasons for it, he must be allowed to emigrate and to seek residence in other countries. Merely because he is a citizen of one country does not deprive him of membership in the human family, nor of citizenship in that universal society, the common, world-wide fellowship of men.

Man's personal dignity involves his right to take an active part in public life, and to make his own contribution to the common welfare. As Pope Pius XII said, "Man is no mere object or inert element in society. He is, rather, its subject, its basis and its purpose; and so must be esteemed."

And, finally, as a human person he is entitled to the legal protection of his rights, a protection which must be effective, unbiased, and strictly just.

All these rights give rise in the same person to corresponding duties. Both rights and duties exist, are protected, and are inviolable by way of the natural law, which in conferring the one imposes the other.

In human society one man's natural right obliges other men to recognize and respect that right. Every basic human right draws its authoritative force from the natural law, which confers it and attaches to it its respective duty. Thus, to claim one's rights and ignore one's duties, or only half fulfill them, is like building a shelter with one hand and tearing it down with the other.

Man's personal dignity requires besides that he enjoy freedom and be able to make up his own mind when he acts. In free association with others, therefore, there is every reason why he should act on his own initiative, be able to express his own convictions and sense of responsibility, and do this freely, not merely in response to the constant pressure of external forces.

A society that is welded together by force is not

human. Far from encouraging the attainment of man's progress and perfection, it is merely an obstacle to his freedom.

Thus, if a society wishes to be well-ordered, creative, and consonant with human dignity, it must be founded on truth. Saint Paul expressed this as follows: "Putting away lying, speak the truth every man with his neighbor, for we are members one of another." And so will it be, if each man acknowledges sincerely his own rights and his own duties toward others.

But further, men must love in such a way that they will feel the needs of others as their own, that they will be moved to share their goods with others, and to work that all may enjoy the richness of man's highest intellectual and spiritual values.

And so, human society should be thought of primarily as a spiritual reality.

The foundation of the order which prevails in human society is truth, and justice activates it. The soul and perfection of society is man's love for his brother. Its voice is freedom and it seeks always an equilibrium which grows ever more human in character.

There are, I think, three characteristics of our age. There is first of all a progressive improvement in the economic and social condition of workingmen. The workers began by claiming their rights principally in the economic and social spheres, and then they claimed their political rights as well. Now they seek to gain a share in the wider benefits of society.

Secondly, the part that women are now playing in public life is everywhere apparent. Perhaps it shows a swifter growth among Christian nations, but it is also happening extensively, if more slowly, among nations that are heirs to different traditions and cultures. Women are more conscious of their natural dignity. No longer content with a purely passive role or being considered a kind of fool, they are demanding both in domestic and in public life the rights and duties which belong to them as human persons.

Finally, in this modern age society is evolving on entirely new social and political lines. Since all peoples have either attained political independence or are on the way to attaining it, soon no nation will have dominance over another and none will be subject to a foreign power.

Thus throughout the world men are either the citizens of independent nations or shortly will be. No nation today is content to accept foreign rule. And within the nation itself, the presumed inferiority of certain classes because of their economic and social status, sex, or position in the state and the corresponding superiority complex of other classes are rapidly disappearing.

The conviction today, on the contrary, is that all men are equal in natural dignity. Thus, theoretically at least, racial discrimination is outlawed.

Human society can be neither well-ordered nor prosperous without the presence of leaders legitimately constituted, who preserve its institutions and do all that is necessary to promote the interest of all. They derive authority from God, for, as Saint Paul teaches, "there is no power but from God." In his commentary on this passage, John Chrysostom writes: "What are you saying? Is every ruler appointed by God? No, that is not what I mean, for I am not now talking about individual rulers, but about authority itself. The existence of a ruling authority, the fact that some should command and others obey, and that all things not just happen by chance—this proceeds from the divine wisdom."

But authority is not without limits. Permission to govern is conditioned by authority's agreement to do so in accordance with right reason, and its binding force comes from the moral order, which in turn has God as its origin and end.

Hence, a government which rules solely or mainly

by means of threats and intimidation or promises of reward provides no effective challenge for men to work for the common good. And even if it did, it would certainly be inconsistent with the dignity of free and rational human beings.

Authority is before all else a moral force, and its appeal should be to the individual conscience, to the duty which every man has of voluntarily contributing to the common good.

But since all men are equal in natural dignity, no man has the right to force internal compliance on another. Only God can do that, for He alone scrutinizes and judges the secret counsels of the heart.

The fact that authority comes from God does not mean that men have no power to choose those who are to lead them, or to decide the type of government they want, or to determine the procedure and the limitations of authority.

Since the attainment of the common good is the sole reason for the existence of civil authority, authority must respect its nature and at the same time adapt legislation to the needs of the national situation.

The common good is such that every citizen has the right to share in it, although in different ways, depending on his role, worth, and circumstances.

Hence civil authority must strive to promote the common good in the interest of all, without favoring any individual citizen or category of citizens.

Yet justice and equity can at times demand that this same authority exercise greater care on behalf of the weaker members of society, since they are less capable of defending their own rights and asserting their legitimate interests.

As to what the ideal form of government may be, it seems to me that human nature is best served if the state embodies in its structure a threefold division corresponding to its three main functions. In such a state a precise legal framework is provided, not only for the exercise of power but also for a framework within which the relations between citizens and public officials are expressed. This affords a sure protection to citizens, both in the safeguarding of their rights and in the fulfillment of their duties.

The right of citizens to take part in government offers a new and extensive field for service. In turn civil authority can, from increased contact and discussion with the people, better understand what contributes most effectively to the common good. Where the system allows for a regular succession of public officials, their authority, far from growing old and feeble, takes on a new vitality in keeping with the progressive development of human society.

Such aims and ideals are giving rise to various demands concerning the juridical organization of states. The first is this: that a clear and precisely worded charter of fundamental human rights be formulated and incorporated into the state's general constitution. Secondly, each state must have a public constitution, juridically expressed, which clearly designates the manner of selecting public officials, their reciprocal relations, spheres of competence, and prescribed method of operation. The final demand is that relations between citizens and public authority be described in terms of rights and duties; it must be clear that the principal function of public authorities is to recognize, respect, coordinate, safeguard, and promote citizens' rights and duties.

Nations too are the subjects of reciprocal rights and duties. This my predecessors have constantly taught, and I gladly lend the weight of my own authority to their teaching. Their relationships must be constructed in accordance with the dictates of truth, justice, willing cooperation, and freedom. The same law of nature that governs the life and conduct of individuals must also regulate the relations of political communities with one another.

The ties between nations must be governed by truth. Truth calls for the elimination of every trace of racial discrimination. It follows that all states are by nature equal in dignity. Each of them accordingly has the right to exist, to develop, and to possess the necessary means and accept the primary responsibility for its own development. Each is also legitimately entitled to its good name and to the respect which is its due.

It cannot be denied that some nations possess superior degrees of scientific, cultural and economic development. But they cannot for that reason exert unjust political control over other nations. Such superiority as they possess means only that they have to make a greater contribution to the common cause of social progress.

VII

NATIONS

THE EARTH AND ALL IT contains belong to God. God is the Master, we the inhabitants of the earth. Our duty is to favor that peaceful evolution of peoples which recognizes the rights of one's neighbors, even when this involves personal limitations or renunciation.

Truth further demands an attitude of serene objectivity in the use made by modern scientific methods to promote understanding between nations. A nation may indeed draw attention to the virtues of its way of life, but not to the point where in doing so it violates the principles of truth and justice and injures the reputation of another nation.

99

Since nations have the right to existence, to self-development, to play the leading part in the process of their own development, and the right to their good name, it follows that they are bound to safeguard all such rights effectively and to avoid any action that would violate them. And just as individual men may not seek their own interests in an unjust or harmful way, so too a nation acts criminally if it seeks to improve itself by means which work to the harm of other nations and unjustly oppress them. There is a saying of Saint Augustine which has particular relevance in this context: "Take away justice, and what are kingdoms but mighty bands of robbers?" Every deviation in the history of individual peoples in this matter of peace has been a contradiction, sometimes surreptitious, sometimes overt, of the Gospel.

As nations strive for their own development there can be and often there is a clash of interests. When they arise, they must be settled in a human way, not by force or deceit or trickery. A mutual assessment of the arguments and feelings on both sides, a mature and objective investigation of the situation, and an equitable reconciliation of opposing views—this is what is required. To promote, favor, and accept negotiations, at all levels, is a rule of wisdom and

prudence which calls down the blessing of heaven
and earth.

An instance of this is furnished by that political
trend by which men of similar ethnic background
are anxious for political autonomy and unification
into a single nation. For many reasons this cannot
always be done, and minority peoples are often
obliged to live within the territories of a nation of a
different ethnic origin, with consequent serious
problems. Any attempt to check the vitality and
growth of these ethnic minorities is a flagrant violation of justice; the more so if such efforts are
aimed at their very extinction.

Sometimes, however, these minorities, possibly
in reaction against the hardships of their present
situation, or for historical reasons, tend to exalt ex-
cessively characteristics which are proper to themselves. They even rate them above those human
values which are common to all mankind, as though
the good of the entire human family should be subordinate to the interests of their group.

A more reasonable attitude would be to recognize the advantages which are theirs by reason of
the special situation. Their constant association
with a people of a different culture can help in the
development of their own particular genius and

spirit. Little by little they can absorb into their very
being those virtues which characterize the other nation.

Of its very nature civil authority exists, not to
contain men within the frontiers of their own nations, but primarily to protect the common good of
the nation, which certainly cannot be divorced from
the common good of the entire human family. Relations between nations must be regulated in accordance with the principles of truth and justice.
These relationships can be deepened by the pooling
of material and spiritual resources. In many cases
this can be achieved by a complex of mutual assistance, and it is, in fact, happening in our own day
in the economic, social, political, educational,
health, and athletic spheres—and with beneficial results.

From World War II right up to the present time,
what an abuse there has been of the sacred word
peace. I pay homage to the good will of the many
guides and proclaimers of peace in the world: states-
men, experienced diplomats, and writers. But human efforts in the matter of universal peacemaking
are still far from the point where heaven and earth
meet.

I am deeply distressed to see the quantity of
armaments that have been, and are, manufactured

in the economically more developed countries. This
is a policy which involves a vast outlay of intellectual and material resources. As a result the citizens
of these nations struggle under a heavy burden,
while other countries lack the help they need for
their economic and social development.

Under modern conditions, it is said, peace cannot be assured except on the basis of an equal balance of armaments and thus these must be stock-
piled. If one country increases its military strength,
others do the same. If one country is equipped with
atomic weapons, others consider themselves justified
in producing weapons of equal destructive force.

And so people live in fear. It is difficult for us to
believe that anyone would dare to assume responsibility for launching a war with the death and deso-
lation it would bring to mankind, but it is less difficult to envision it beginning by some chance or
unforeseen circumstance. Moreover, even though
the power of modern weapons does act as a deterrent, there is reason to fear that the testing of nuclear devices for war weapons can, if continued,
lead to serious danger for various forms of life on
earth.

Hence justice, right reason, and a sense of man's
dignity insist on an end to the arms race. The stock-
piles of armaments which have been built up in

various countries must be reduced jointly and simultaneously. Nuclear weapons must be banned. A
general agreement must be reached on a suitable
disarmament program, with an effective system of
mutual control.

Since the men of our time have not completely
carried out the conditions of peace, the result has
been that God's paths to peace have no point of
encounter with those of man. Hence there is the ab-
normal situation of this postwar period which has
created, as it were, two blocs, with all their uneasiness. There is not a state of war, but neither is there
that peace which nations so ardently desire.

It is impossible to stop the arms race, or to reduce
armaments, or—and this is the main thing—ultimately to abolish them entirely unless this process
of disarmament is thorough and complete, and
reaches men's very souls.

All must sincerely cooperate in seeking to banish
fear and the anxious expectation of war from men's
minds. But this requires that the law on which peace
is based today must be replaced by an altogether
different one—namely, the law of mutual trust.
True and lasting peace among nations cannot be
constructed on the joint possession of an equal supply of armaments! I know that what we hope can be
achieved, because not only does common sense call

for it but it is itself a worthy and beneficent goal.

And it must always be remembered that without God's help no house can be solidly built, nor is there any city that can rely for its defense only on the vigilance of men. Peace is the happy legacy of those who keep the divine law. "Much peace have they who love thy law."

For its part, the will for peace is simply the sincere determination to respect the eternal laws of God, to conform oneself to His commandments and to follow His paths—in short, to abide in truth. This is the glory which God expects to receive from man. "Peace among men of good will."

Therefore I pray God that world leaders may carefully weigh and consider the causes of dissension and strive in good faith to remove them. They must, above all, realize that war can have only one result and thus cannot bring about any desired result save this—vast ruins everywhere. The laws which regulate the state and society and which bind together nations and classes of society must speak to the needs of today's men. They must be mindful of the eternal laws which come from God and are the foundation and hinge of all government. Finally, they must be ever aware that the individual souls of men are created by God and destined to possess Him.

Men today are slowly growing in awareness that any disputes which may arise between nations must be resolved by negotiation and agreement, not by recourse to arms. The terrifying and destructive force of modern weapons is responsible for such awareness. In an age of atomic power it no longer makes sense to defend the principle that war is a fit instrument with which to repair the violation of justice.

Nevertheless, I continue to be hopeful that by mutual contact and by a policy of negotiation nations will come to acknowledge the ties that bind them together as men. My hope, too, is that once the legitimate aspirations of people for liberty and independence have been satisfied, the rich will help the poor, the strong will help the weak, the more advanced nations will hold out a helping hand to the less developed, and, in the end, all will feel themselves brothers, for all are sons of the same loving Father Who is in heaven.

Today no state living in isolation from the rest can adequately pursue its own interests, nor can it develop as it should. The prosperity and progress of any nation is in part consequence, and in part cause, of the prosperity and progress of all other nations.

Mutual relationships of nations have undergone

significant changes. Concern for the universal common good heightens awareness of problems of the utmost gravity, complexity, and urgency—especially as regards the preservation of the security and peace of the whole world.

But it must be said in all candor that the structure of political life in the modern world and the influence of the governments of the various nations are today incapable of promoting the common good of all peoples.

This common good raises problems which affect all peoples, and which cannot be solved except by an authority with power, organization, and means equal in scope to these problems, and with a global sphere of action. Consequently the moral order itself demands the establishment of some such supranational form of public authority.

But this authority endowed with world-wide power and adequate means for achieving the universal common good cannot be imposed by force. It must be set up with the consent of all nations. To be effective, it must operate with fairness, absolute impartiality, and dedication to the common good of all peoples. Were such a universal authority to be forcibly imposed by the more powerful nations it would inevitably arouse suspicion of its being an instrument of the few or the puppet of a single nation. Its influence and the effectiveness of its activity would thus be undermined. For although nations may differ widely in material progress and military strength, they are sensitive concerning their juridic equality and the value of their own way of life. They are right, therefore, in their reluctance to submit to an authority imposed by force, established without their cooperation, or not accepted of their own accord.

As the common good of individual nations cannot be determined without reference to the human person, so the same is true of the common good of all states taken together. Hence the public authority of the world community must likewise have as its special aim the recognition, safeguarding, and promotion of the rights of the human person. This can be done by direct action, if need be, or by establishing conditions throughout the world whereby the heads of individual nations could more easily fulfill their obligations to their citizens.

The principle of subsidiarity which governs the relations between public authorities and individuals, families, and intermediate societies in a single nation must also apply to the relations between the public authority of the world community and the public authority of each nation. This universal authority must evaluate and find a solution to economic, social, political, and cultural problems which affect the universal common good and which, because of their gravity, vastness, and urgency, must be considered too difficult for the rulers of individual states to solve with any degree of success.

But it is not for the universal authority to limit the sphere of action of the individual nations, or to arrogate any of their functions to itself. Its essential purpose is to create world conditions in which the leaders of each nation, its citizens, and its intermediate groups can carry out their tasks, fulfill their duties, and claim their rights with greater security.

It is my fervent wish that the United Nations may be able progressively to adapt its structure and methods of operation to the magnitude and nobility of its tasks. May the day come when this organization can effectively protect the personal rights of every human being. I speak of those rights which are his because of his dignity as a human person, and which are therefore universal, inviolable, and inalienable.

As long as we live in exile on this earth, our peace and happiness will be imperfect. Such peace is not completely untroubled and serene; it is a peace which is active, not calm and motionless. It is a peace that is ever at war. It wars with every sort of error, including that which falsely wears the face of truth; it struggles against vice, against enemies of

the soul, of whatever description, who can weaken,
blemish, or destroy our innocence or faith.

This is why our divine Redeemer left *His* peace
with us, gave *His* peace to us.

The peace, then, that we must seek, that we must
strive to achieve with all the means at our disposal,
must make no concessions to error, must compromise in no way with proponents of falsehood. It
must discourage all discord. Those who adhere to
this peace must be ready to renounce their own interests and advantages for the sake of truth and
justice, according to the words "Seek first the Kingdom of God and His justice." For there is only one
cause of discord, disagreement, and dissension: ignorance of the truth, or, what is worse, rejection of
the truth once it has been sought and found.

My service as a chaplain in the hospitals during
World War I is something I will never forget. In the
groans of the sick and the wounded I heard the universal longing for that supreme good of humanity,
peace. Then more than ever before I felt how deeply
rooted is the desire for peace in man and especially
in someone like a soldier, who trusts that he is laying the groundwork for the future through his personal sacrifice and often the laying down of his life.

The edifice of peace must be built day by day,

and on solid foundations. *Pacem in Terris* is meant
to be my Easter gift for the year of our Lord 1963.
It is an expression of the desire that inflames my soul
as shepherd of the Church, a reflection of the heart
of Christ. "He is our peace," says the Apostle Paul,
"and, coming, He preached peace to you that were
afar off; and peace to them that were near. For by
Him we have access both in one Spirit to the
Father."

Today, even as yesterday, the Church summons
men unceasingly to unity in love. This is the message I have to speak clearly to all men through the
encyclical *Pacem in Terris*. I am pleased that it
should appear on this day when Christ said, "Love
one another." What I wanted to do more than all
else was to shout to the people of today a great call
to love. May they be quick to acknowledge the
common origin that makes them brothers and unites
them. May a new vitality be given to governments
by the love that will penetrate the hearts of men.
May it help them to accept God's presence in history, His laws, and their practical consequences, and
make for concrete application. May all their actions
be inspired by the spirit of obedience to a law which
transcends the life of individuals. In this spirit may
they not overlook anything which will enhance the

growth of the human person and ensure a social
order solidly rooted in truth, justice, peace, and
liberty!

This is my prayer. May peace, the daughter of
gentleness and good will, establish a lasting rule
among the nations.

VIII

REFLECTIONS

God Has Called upon Us to Heal Our
Brothers, Not to Frighten Them

THE MESSAGE OF our Savior, Christ, was an announcement of joy; it was the joyful good news. It is a mistake to think of Christianity, as did many thinkers and poets of the past, as something lugubrious and sad. No! Christianity is joy. Joy in right order, in peace with God, with oneself, and with one's neighbor.

How great is the wisdom of our God, Who even in the midst of our time of severest testing shows the depths of His mercy to us, poor creatures that we are.

The wisdom of man, the wisdom of the Christian,

113

is to make every effort to free himself from sadness.

Seek joy, sounding always a note of sincerity, of rectitude. Avoid all that is lying and evasion, in order that your life may be a jet of living water which will flow into eternal life.

A truly great and valiant soul never becomes a prey to melancholy, even in the hour of its greatest tribulation.

Christianity is not the mass of restrictions which the unbeliever imagines. On the contrary, it is peace, joy, love, and life, which, like the hidden pulse of nature in early spring, is ever being renewed.

The holy religion we profess is not an empty exercise of gestures, rites, and exterior practices, sometimes even superstitions. But it is a knowledge and profound conviction of an eternal and divine doctrine that enlightens the civilization of which we are proud. Above all, it is an affirmation of justice and charity compressed and lived in the intimacy of each one's life, and in the wider world of his contacts and friendships.

When the Gospel message was preached by Christ, only a small number of men received it. With the passage of time the number grew. In the twenty centuries which have passed, millions have preferred the poetry of the Cross to the delights of the world. The world today shows signs of betrayal and decadence, but I love to recall that in these years which mark our time millions and millions of men and women have received the invitation of the Cross and have given themselves to the service of God, of Church, and of their fellow men.

Be watchful and delicate of conscience. Do not disperse your fervor in a variety of devotions while there is still such a great need for learning perfectly, not only to recite but also to practice the Lord's Prayer.

Experience has taught me that the multiplication of laws and decrees can be stifling. Instead of life, all that remains is the dead letter of the law.

Our trust, our certainty of victory in the name of Jesus, does not mean that once a trial is behind us we can turn over in bed and go back to sleep. God wishes to save us, but this he will not do without our cooperation.

Life is a duty to be fulfilled, not a pleasure to be acquired and enjoyed.

Do not try to be one of those who are always hailing the beginning of a new era as if, before they appeared on the stage of life, all had been emptiness or chaos. Before us came our parents, and the generations that have preceded us have left such evidence of their strength, and of their conquest of truth and the good, as to make us fear that we could never equal either their merit or their glory.

Do not walk through time without leaving worthy evidence of your passage.

Be always willing to begin, ready always to rejuvenate yourself spiritually.

It is not my way to call attention to the threat of divine punishment. I prefer, rather, the simple affirmation of what I have found in the eyes and on the lips and in the whole way of life of those dear people among whom I grew up and to whom I feel myself forever intimately joined.

God has called upon us to enlighten consciences, not to confuse or coerce them. God asks us to speak with simplicity, not to complicate matters or to flatter the tastes of an audience.

God has called upon us to heal our brothers, not to frighten them!

The Church has always opposed error, and often condemned it with the utmost severity. Today, however, it prefers mercy to severity. It believes that our needs are best served by explaining more fully the purport of its doctrines, rather than by publishing condemnations.

Using the power that only love can give, go to everybody. Go wherever there are minds to be enlightened, wills to be strengthened, energies to be channeled toward good. Wherever there are tears to be dried, doubts to be dispelled, solitudes to be filled, be there. Approach with meekness and patience your estranged brothers, who may hide, behind the screen of their negations, a wounded heart that needs love and understanding. Try to convince them that hatred is not a solution of their problems, nor the triumph of anti-Christian ideologies the secret for changing the world. Show them, rather, that the willing, consistent, and determined practice of the teachings of the Gospel, even at the cost of personal sacrifice, is the solution and the secret.

The Christ is the most precious inheritance of the ages. He lives ever with us, not seen, often forgotten, often a sign of contradiction, but always with us. He joins us as the unknown pilgrim on our way, with us in our uncertainty, our suffering, our need.

Above all, one must always be ready for the Lord's surprise moves. Although he treats his loved ones well, he generally likes to test them with all sorts of trials such as bodily infirmities, bitterness of soul, and sometimes opposition so powerful as to weary and wear out the life of His servant.

Life holds many consolations, but it is always a voyage, and the traveling tires and weakens.

The Christian life is a sacrifice.

This, and nothing else, is the reality: without discipline man is not man. Without penance a Christian is not a Christian.

Let the Cross be the source of your strength, the inspiration of your prayers, and the secret of your peace.

There are two gates to Paradise: innocence and penance. Who among us can expect to find the first of these wide open? But we may be sure of the other: Jesus passed through it, bearing His Cross in atonement for our sins, and He invites us to follow Him. But following Him means doing penance.

I will not try to save my soul by defacing an original painting, which has its own merits, in order to become an unsuccessful copy of someone else whose character is entirely different from mine.

It is commonly believed that the Pope's language, even in ordinary conversations, ought to savor of the mysterious and the circumspect. But it is more in keeping with the example of Jesus to maintain attractive simplicity.

Simplicity often generates, if not contempt, at least lack of respect in the pompous. But they do not matter very much, even if they are able to inflict some humiliation by their opinions or attitude. It is they who will be confounded in the end.

What bitterness is caused by a rough, abrupt, or

impatient manner! Sometimes the fear of being un-
derestimated tempts us to give ourselves airs and
assert ourselves a little. But this is contrary to my
nature. To be simple, with no affectations, requires
no effort from me. This is a great gift that the Lord
has bestowed on me. I want to preserve it and to be
worthy of it.

Here is the Christian perspective on peace: We
are made for peace and not for war. The life of a
Christian must be a constant effort to gain and hold
peace, an unflagging directing of all his energies to
this end.

Fewer words on the obligations of others; greater
attention to ourselves and to drawing from our times
whatever will make us good, dear to God and to
men.

The truth. Always the truth. Speak it and write it
with respect and care. Speak it to others as you
would have it spoken to you. And do it always in
such a way as not to offend the sacred meaning of
divine or human law, of innocence, of justice, or of
peace.

To be honest with the Lord, to know how to
pray with humility and absolute confidence—this is
what matters.

Whatever the program, for whatever purpose or
cause, if love is not there, then beware. Without love

there can be temporary successes, but with time they crumble.

Above all it is necessary to put down the I and find one's values and identity in men.

A spotless life is always poetry and freshness, always happiness and enthusiasm, always the entrancing conqueror of souls.

I have kept alive devotion to humility and to its practice. This does not mean I feel nothing when it seems that some lack of regard has been shown me. But I even rejoice about it before God as an exercise of patience.

Over and above all the opinions and parties that stir up and afflict society and the whole of mankind rises the Gospel. The Pope reads it and, along with the bishops, comments on it. Together they act not as men promoting worldly interests, but, rather, as inhabitants of that City of Peace from which comes the divine rule that can guide the earthly city and the whole world.

As a matter of fact, this is what sensible men are looking for from the Church, and nothing else.

To Christ Jesus be the glory. Do not fear for His holy Church. He conserves it and maintains it. To difficulties, to the storms of the times, respond with the calm of the Gospel.

The re-establishment of Catholicism in its fullness

and perfection will be the most important event of modern times.

The Catholic Church leaves many questions open. It does this to the extent that matters are not absolutely certain. Far from jeopardizing the Church's unity, controversies, as John Henry Cardinal Newman has remarked, can actually pave the way for its attainment.

Discussion can lead to fuller and deeper understanding of religious truths; when one idea strikes against another, there may be a spark.

It is perfectly legitimate to make a clear distinction between a false philosophy of the nature, the origin, and the purpose of men and the world and economic, social, cultural, and political activities, even when these are inspired by that philosophy.

The philosophic formula does not change once it has been set down in precise terms, but the activities themselves clearly cannot avoid being influenced by the changing conditions in which they take place. Besides, who can deny the possible existence of good and commendable elements in these activities, elements which conform to the dictates of right reason and are an expression of man's lawful hopes?

It is proper to distinguish between error and the one who holds it, including those who err as a result of inadequate knowledge, in matters of religion or

of ethical standards. A man who has fallen into
error does not cease to be a man, nor does he forfeit
his personal dignity; and that should be remembered. Besides, man never loses his capacity to reject
error and embrace truth.

My first contacts with the lowly and the great;
charitable visits here and there; my meekness and
humility in approaching and clarifying ideas, and in
giving fervent encouragement; the Lenten visits to
new parishes; the unexpected success of the diocesan
synod; the drawing closer of the Papacy to the whole
of Christendom through the creation of cardinals
and of bishops from every nation and every race and
color; and now the vast movement of the Ecumenical Council—all this confirms the wisdom of the
principle of waiting to express with faith, with
modesty, and with trusting fervor the inspiration
which the grace of Christ provides.

I say with the Psalmist: Your right hand has sustained, me, Lord; Your merciful care has lifted me
up. This is the mystery of my life. Do not look else-
where for an explanation. Not our will but the will
of God is our peace.

For the man who always keeps his trusting gaze
fixed on God, there are no surprises—not even the
surprise of death, of that death which is holy, because it is the vestibule to glory.

To expect everything here on earth, from this world which is simply a way station or a resting ground, is a profound deception.

Blessed Jesus, God and man, I confirm my consecration to You for life, for death, and for eternity.

A GOOD TIME TO DIE

*I Have No Right to Look Forward to a
Long Road to Travel as Pope*

THE MEMORY I HAVE of my life is
gladdened by all the grace the Lord has given me.
Yet I have cooperated poorly. My response has been
in no way proportionate to the gifts I have received.
It is a mystery that makes me tremble and at the
same time moves me deeply.

"Simplicity of heart and speech"! The older I
grow the more clearly I experience the dignity and
the beauty of simplicity in thought, conduct, and
speech. The desire grows to simplify all that is com-
plicated and to reduce everything to its ultimate
content and clarity, without wrapping things up in

trimmings and artificial turns of thought and phrase. "To be simple with prudence"—the motto is John Chrysostom's.

Every so often, during the recitation of the Rosary, along with the familiar intentions I add others. At those times I go back over the course of my life. I pray for Bergamo, for the dear people of Bulgaria, for the Turks and the Greeks. I see once again the eight years of my stay among the French, who have been so good to me and whom I continue to love. I see once again Venice, my Venice, which is always on my lips and in my heart. And here I am, here, close to St. Peter's and the Lateran.

In the early days of my pontificate, I didn't fully realize all that it meant to be the Bishop of Rome and, as a result, the shepherd of the universal Church. Then slowly, week by week, a full understanding came. And I have felt at home, as if I had never done anything else in my whole life.

My poor life, now such a long one, has unwound itself as easily as a ball of string, under the sign of simplicity and purity. The Lord caused me to be born of poor folk, and He has seen to all my needs. I have left it to Him. As a young priest I was struck by the motto "Obedience and Peace" of Cesare Baronius, and I have left everything to God and have allowed myself to be led in perfect obedience to the plans of Providence. Truly, "the will of God is my peace."

When I look back over fifty years of priesthood I experience a blend of confusion, of gratitude, and of shame. Gratitude, of course, for the graces which sustained me, shame for my numerous offenses and negligences. The remembrance of the past does not in any way diminish my vision of the present. And for me the present, illumined by the will of the Master, is my "venerable age."

"Give me more light as evening falls." O Lord, I am now in the evening of my life. Three quarters of my contemporaries have passed over to the far shore. So I too must always be ready for the great moment. The thought of death does not alarm me. Old age and infirmity are infallible messengers of approaching death. Surely it is a signal grace from the Lord to be able to live a long life. And I, who begin to enjoy the loving caresses of this grace, know that the Lord more than compensates us for the passage of the years with greater clarity of vision, and with spiritual serenity.

The hour set for the visit of sister death is absolute, it is the hour of the Lord.

How much time the Lord will give me to work and to serve Him in His children I do not know, nor do I care. I am ever ready to live and to die.

My attitude is like that of Saint Martin: he was not afraid to die, but neither did he refuse to live.

I must always be ready to die, even suddenly, and to live for as long as the Lord may be pleased to leave me here below. Yes, always. On the threshold of my eightieth year, I must stay ready to die or to live. I must be and I want to be truly what I am called everywhere, and what is my principal title: "Holy Father."

Having entered upon and now completed my eightieth year doesn't really disturb me; instead it keeps me calm and confident. I continue the same way as always: I desire nothing more nor less than what the Lord continues to give me. I thank Him and I bless Him every day. I am ready for anything. By the grace of the Lord, I have not yet entered into extreme old age, but I find myself at the door. And so I must keep ready for this last stage of my life where limitations and sacrifices are waiting for me. O Jesus, here I am ready to extend my hands that are now weak and trembling, to let others help me get dressed and support me along the way.

Old age, which is a great gift of the Lord, must be for me a source of serene joy, and a reason for trusting day by day in the Lord Himself. I turn to Him now as a child turns to the open arms of his father.

Some time ago I resolved to have always in mind a reverent expectation of death, this *joy* which ought to be my soul's last smile when it departs from this life. There is no point in burdening others by speaking frequently of this; but I must always think of it, because the consideration of death, when it has become a familiar thought, is good and useful to restrain vanity and to give a sense of moderation and calm to everything. This serenity of mine, this readiness to depart and appear before the Lord when He calls, seems to me to be such a sign of trust and love as to deserve from Jesus, Whose Vicar on earth I am called, the final gesture of His mercy. No, I do not weep, and I do not even desire to live my life over again so as to do better. I entrust to the Lord's mercy whatever I have done, however badly, and I look to the future, brief or long as it may be, because I want it to be holy and a source of holiness to others.

As for what the world may say, let us "rejoice and do well" and let the sparrows twitter.

The good wishes for a long life, for prosperity, and for a happy resolution of all my work, expressed with such goodness and tenderness by all, touch me profoundly. But they do not keep me from thinking of that other shore which awaits me.

The mystery of our life is in the hands of God.

All that matters is to walk in justice and sanctity in the eyes of Heaven and of our conscience, with pure and loving action. So let us continue moving slowly toward Him, as if He stood waiting with open arms.

I know that I am close to the end of my life. When I look back and see the faces of those who have gone before me, those who were dear to me, and when I remember them and the conversations we used to have, I feel myself profoundly moved. The sense of aloneness which could assail me is tempered and sweetened by the thought of the new generation, who join their vibrancy to the life of those further along the road we journey. Thus joined, we all work together in shaping the times to come.

Old age is not extraneous to life and to the beat of the new generations that rise around us and even do so with an air of having more to teach than to learn. They still respect us and are proud of us.

I tremble when I think of how the Lord will judge me, looking at me by the light of His lantern. But when I ask myself what more I can do to please the Lord, I find no other answer than this: continue under obedience as you are doing now; do your ordinary tasks day after day, without overanxiety, without ostentation, but always trying to do them with greater fervor and perfection.

In Psalm 89, perhaps the oldest of the Psalms

because it is attributed to Moses and not to David, it says that the ordinary length of a man's life is seventy years, and for him who is strong in his health eighty. But even eighty years are few in the sight of God, and since the life of every man is in the hands of God it is proper, it is beautiful, it is edifying for the children to pray for further years for their Father. We are no longer in the days of Pope Innocent III (1216) who wrote: "Few now live to their fortieth year, and fewer still live to be sixty."

Youth is good when we avail ourselves of the advantages it offers, but old age is better. There is joy in old age. Let us enjoy it.

O Jesus, here I am before you. I am old now, at the end of my service, at the end of my life. Keep me very close to your heart, and make its beat one with mine. I would like to feel myself inseparably bound to You with a chain of gold made up of fine and delicate links.

This life of mine that is turning toward its sunset could not be better dissolved than in my concentrating completely on Jesus. After all the graces I have received during my long life, there is nothing more that I want.

Before I die, I think the Lord intends for me, in order to empty and purify me for entrance into His joy, some great suffering and affliction of body and spirit. If and when great tribulation comes upon me, may I accept it well. And if this be a while yet, then may I continue to drink the blood of Jesus and to accept that combination of small or great tribulations that the Lord in His goodness may choose to set around it.

I have always been deeply impressed, and still am, by that little Psalm 130, which says: "O Lord, my heart is not proud, nor are my eyes haughty; I busy not myself with great things, nor with things too sublime for me." Yet I distrust my resistance to physical pain. My only wish is that my life should end in a holy manner. I tremble at the thought of having to bear pain, responsibilities, or difficulties beyond my strength, but I trust in the Lord.

I am aware of the beginning of a certain disturbance in my body that must be natural for an old man. I bear with it quietly, even if it does give me a little annoyance at times and even in spite of the fact that it makes me fear that it may be growing worse. It is not pleasant to think about it much, but I feel prepared for anything.

I came away from Easter content, but actually not feeling well as far as my stomach is concerned. Today a little rest at home, but with a great deal of distraction. A long audience with Cardinal Testa.

Disturbances continue so as to make me think seriously about my condition.

This morning the peace prize of the Stephen Balzan Foundation was conferred upon me in the Sala Regia of the Vatican. May the Almighty Lord grant me a peaceful night and a perfect end.

This morning for the third time I rested content with receiving Holy Communion in bed, instead of enjoying the celebration of Holy Mass. Patience, patience! Still I could not refuse to receive the farewell visit of Cardinal Wyszynski, primate of Poland, with four of his bishops who are on their way back to their homeland. The rest of the day in bed, with several particularly painful episodes. I am helped, and always with great charity, by those who are close to me.

On the point of presenting myself before the One and Triune Lord Who created me, redeemed me, chose me to be His priest and bishop, and covered me with unending graces, I entrust my poor soul to His mercy. I humbly ask pardon for my sins and deficiencies. I offer Him the little good, imperfect though it be, that with His aid I have succeeded in doing, for His glory, for the service of Holy Church and for the world. I beg Him finally to receive me, like a good and kind father, with His saints into eternal happiness.

I profess once again with all my heart my entire Christian and Catholic faith, my adherence and subjection to the Holy Apostolic and Roman Church.

The sense of my own littleness and nothingness has always been my good companion, keeping me humble and calm. It has given me the joy of living to the best of my ability a life of obedience and charity for others and for the interests of the Kingdom of Jesus, my Lord and my all. To Him be all glory; for me and my merit, His mercy.

I ask pardon of those whom I have unknowingly offended, of all to whom I have not been an example of goodness. I feel that I have nothing to forgive anyone, for all who have known and dealt with me, including those who have offended me, I regard solely as brothers and benefactors, to whom I am grateful and for whom I pray and always will pray.

Born poor, but of honorable and humble people, I am particularly happy to die poor. In accordance with the various demands and circumstances of my life, I have given away, for the benefit of the poor and of the Holy Church that nurtured me, all that came into my hands—which was little enough, as a matter of fact—during the years as priest and bishop.

I thank God for this grace of poverty which I vowed in my youth, poverty of spirit and real poverty. This grace has sustained me in never asking for anything, neither positions, money, nor favors—never, not for myself and not for my relatives or friends. At my death I will not lack the tribute that so honored the holiness of Pius X: born poor and died poor.

To my beloved family I can leave only a whole-hearted and special blessing. I ask them all to maintain that fear of God that always made them so dear and beloved to me, simple and modest, without my ever feeling ashamed of them. This is their true title of honor. I have sought to help them at times in their more serious needs, as one poor man does with another. But I have never sought to raise them above an honorable and accepted poverty. I pray and always will pray for their prosperity. I am happy to see in the new, vigorous offshoots of the family that strength and loyalty to their fathers' religious traditions which will always be their endowment. My fervent wish is that none of my relatives and dear ones may miss the joy of our last eternal reunion.

The goodness directed toward me by all whom I met along my path made my life serene. As I face death, I recall each and every one—those who have preceded me and those who survive me and who will follow me. May they pray for me.

I await and will accept with simplicity and joy

the arrival of sister death in all the circumstances of her coming.

This bed is an altar. An altar requires a victim. I am ready. I have before me the clear vision of my soul, of my priesthood, of the Council, of the universal Church.

The Lord is quite right in adding the Cross to the signs of mercy which He has shown me, especially during these last months. I am at peace. My desire has been always to do the will of God, always, always. I pray for the Church, for children, for priests and bishops that they may be holy, for the whole world.

Having come forth from the poverty and nothingness of Sotto il Monte, I tried never to separate myself from it. What grace the Lord has granted me!

I want to die without knowing whether I own anything of my own. Poverty has often embarrassed me, especially when I was not able to help my own who were very poor, or some brother priest. But I have never regretted it. I am poor, thank God, and I mean to die poor.

The Council: God knows that I have opened my soul to this great inspiration with simplicity. Will He let me finish it? May He be blessed. Will He not let me finish it? I will see its successful conclusion from heaven.

I consider it a sign of great mercy shown to me by the Lord Jesus that He continues to give me His peace.

O Lord Jesus, continue to have mercy upon me, a poor sinner, so that I may feel sure of Your great and eternal pardon.

I remember all and will pray for all. The dear people of Rome! I will always love them, and from heaven I will go on protecting them.

At the moment for saying farewell or, better still, *arrivederci,* I once more remind everyone of what counts most in life: the blessed Christ, His Holy Church, His Gospel; and in the Gospel, above all, the Our Father.

I have read back over what I wrote in my book in the midst of the World War in 1916: the last days of Bishop Radini, his final invocation, "Peace, peace." I would like it to be my last prayer as Pope, too, as the humble Pope John.

My children, my brothers, *arrivederci*—until we meet again.

EPILOGUE

THIS VOLUME by Pope John XXIII in *Credo Per-*
spectives reflects that unity of purpose, that capacity
for self-transcendence, that structural indwelling between man and his work which this series seeks to
define and which so exquisitely reveals the life of
one of the most eminent Popes in the history of the
Church. He risked the threat of theological syncre-
tism by proclaiming the unity of all men under one
God.

The enthusiasm for the person and the work of
Pope John that swept the world at the time of his
death was an extraordinary phenomenon. Neither

Pope John's personality, his simplicity, his humility, nor the fact that he had convened the Council and appealed for unity can fully explain this phenomenon. It is true, of course, that the acclamation which greeted his last encyclical, his *Pacem in Terris,* was largely responsible for the fervor surrounding the Pope's last days. Nevertheless, that is not the key to the mystery. It does not explain the affection, the love, that Pope John inspired in men everywhere.

John XXIII appeared as the symbol of peace in a world on the edge of the abyss of total war, a peace pursued not in order to promote some policy or some revolutionary ideology, but a peace pursued as a good in itself and as an imperative of human nature for survival.

The spontaneous veneration of John is evidence of a distracted, impotent yearning in modern man. And Pope John's genius consisted in his ability to sense this fundamental anguish in the human soul, to express it in its simplest terms and to respond to it with absolute generosity, with the essence of the Gospel meaning.

A myth has been created. Rarely, indeed, in history has the papacy enjoyed such profound prestige. One need only remember what Chateaubriand stated in his *Mémoires d'Outre-Tombe* about the Popes he had known in Rome, or the odium in which Pius IX was held among non-Catholics at the time of his death. Long past also are the days when Protestant polemics painted the Pope as Antichrist and papal Rome as the scarlet woman of the Apocalypse.

Roncalli was the son of Christian peasants and far from denying his origins, he emphasized them. On January 23, 1927, he wrote to his parents on the occasion of their golden wedding:

I find a special cause of thankfulness to the Lord, not only in his having preserved you in such good health after fifty years, but also because all your family has kept that spirit of simplicity, of poverty borne as an honor instead of a burden, of fear of the Lord, of complete unpretentiousness in the face of the world, which is a cause both of tranquility and Peace as long as this earthly life endures, and a pledge of eternal joy in the future. I am happy to think that your children are firmly decided not to change their ways but to raise their children as you have raised yours.

Pope John was totally without ambition. In a letter to a friend who had been disappointed by failures, he wrote:

We were made for the splendor of celestial glory. If the Lord also grants us a little honor on earth, it is of no consequence and quickly fades unless it is of God. If, on the other hand, the Lord has willed that the value of our life should be altogether hidden in Him, it would be ridiculous to seek anything else. The ambitious are the most ridiculous and the most wretched creatures on earth.

John had a horror of ecclesiastical bureaucracy. He entered the Vatican diplomatic service out of obedience, without seeking it, without working his way up to it in the usual manner. From Sofia, on January 3, 1932, he wrote to a friend:

You were so right not to give up the exercise of the priestly ministry. Oh, how I envy you that! I hope the Lord will one day take into account the sacrifice I have had to impose on myself in that regard. Oh, how poor is the life of a bishop or a priest who is reduced to being no more than a diplomat or a bureaucrat.

The basis of John's spirituality was adoration and the joyous, loving acceptance of God's will as revealed in events.

This spiritual depth gave John an unfailing inner peace which, as Pope, he was able to communicate to others and which pervaded all his thoughts and all his deeds. His episcopal metaphor, which epitomized his discourse, he borrowed from Baronius: *Obedientia et pax.*

Yet John, so misunderstood when he was nuncio in Paris and of whom the best that could be then said was that nothing could be expected from his reign, was the very one to give the Church an unanticipated forward thrust. As the eminent theologian Karl Rahner has said, *"Der Übergangspapst Johannes XXIII vollzog den Übergang der Kirche in die Zukunft."* "The transitional Pope John XXIII effected the transition of the Church into the future."

That John demythologized the papacy is self-evident. But by virtue of his simplicity, his apostolic nature, his transparent humility, he succeeded in humanizing the papacy as well. It is striking to note that John XXIII, as Pope, received an affectionate veneration that he failed to achieve when he was nuncio in Paris.

What distinguishes his pontificate is the Vatican Council and the twofold impulse he bestowed upon it: unity of Christendom and *aggiornamento*. It was his historical studies of Saint Carlo Borromeo's reforms that convinced John of the importance of synods in the Church. As a humble and apostolic man, his fundamental concern was not with the prestige of the papacy nor with the preservation of the absolute centrality of the powerful Curia, but rather with the greater good of the universal Church. In the mind and heart of John the demands of the Holy Ghost, the desires of Christ, the scandal of disunity among Christians, and, in fact, among those of all faiths, had greater force than the arguments of men. Inspired with this faith, John XXIII and, with him, another man of God, Cardinal Bea, who was theologically better equipped than the Pope, in the space of a few months transformed the entire ambience of relations between Christians and non-Christians. In his discourse of October 11, 1962, at the opening of the Council, Pope John pointed to two aspects of such an *aggiornamento*. He wanted the Church to abandon the negative, defensive position it had maintained since the Reformation and particularly since the emergence at the end of the seventeenth century of a formidable anti-Christian and anti-religious philosophy. He desired the Church to speak to modern man in a language he could understand, and he recommended a new formulation of the ancient and immutable message of Catholicism.

Pope John was well aware that modern man does not preoccupy himself with questions concerning the relation of Scripture to tradition in the way the fourth-century Greeks threw themselves into the argument of *homoousios* or *homoiousios*. He merely desired that the light of the Gospel and the countenance of Almighty God shine on the face and problems of mankind.

"We must give time time," he was fond of saying—this man who at eighty years of age was inaugurating a great new epoch in the Western world, in Christianity; ecumenizing its spirit, invigorating its substance, and emphasizing again the dynamic, revolutionary character of the Christian faith, its meaning for history and the human person, as opposed to the static detachment of the religions of the East.

Such was Pope John XXIII, at once simple and complex, traditionalist by temperament and yet a

creator of new forms. He refused to split the God-
head: he overcame separation. In his lifetime he
became a legend, and after his death a myth has
been born, one pervaded by a deep truth. John was
a man of God. Spontaneously, without seeking it,
in the midst of the baroque splendor of the Vatican,
he found the way into the hearts and souls of all
mankind, of all faiths and all creeds. For in him all
humanity was reflected and merged as wave with
water, flame with fire, man with God.

R.N.A.